THE PAUL DEBATE

Critical Questions for Understanding the Apostle

N. T. Wright

Originally published in the United States of America in 2015
by Baylor University Press, Waco, Texas

First published in Great Britain in 2016

Society for Promoting Christian Knowledge
36 Causton Street
London SW1P 4ST
www.spck.org.uk

The author and publisher have made every effort to ensure that the external website
and email addresses included in this book are correct and up to date at the time
of going to press. The author and publisher are not responsible for the
content, quality or continuing accessibility of the sites.

British Library Cataloguing-in-Publication Data
A catalogue record for this book is available from the British Library

ISBN 978 – 0 –281– 07411–2
eBook ISBN 978 – 0 –281– 07647–5

First printed in Great Britain by Ashford Colour Press
Subsequently digitally printed in Great Britain

eBook by Graphicraft Limited, Hong Kong

Produced on paper from sustainable forests

Contents

PREFACE

Many colleagues and friends have read my book *Paul and the Faithfulness of God* (*PFG*). They have kindly responded with comments, blogs, criticisms, and in several cases published reviews. A quick survey of those already published reviews reads like a Who's Who of current Anglophone New Testament studies—Barclay, Bockmuehl, de Boer, Brown, Campbell, Dunn, Fredriksen, Gathercole, Gaventa, Gorman, Hurtado, McKnight, Moo, Schreiner, Starling, Tilling, and Witherington. (A volume is in preparation for the WUNT series from Tübingen, which will include essays by scholars from other backgrounds as well, together with my response to them specifically.) The list is as scary as it is gratifying. I wish to express my thanks to them all, even if in some cases their reviews have been unflattering. I should also acknowledge that several of the reviews (those of Barclay, de Boer, Campbell, Fredriksen, and Gaventa come particularly to mind) have made me think not just about what I have tried to say but how I have tried to say it. I fully understand that my writing style, for which many readers have been grateful, can also be easily misunderstood—though I suspect there remains real difficulty with what I say as much as with how I have said it. But I remain grateful for searching reviews that have named particular issues and invited me to reconsider. Scholarship is always a work in progress, and a collaborative one at that. As Ernst Käsemann said about his debate with Krister Stendahl, mutual discussion is an obligation upon us all. I am deeply in my reviewers' debt, as I hope the pages that follow will indicate. A list of these reviews appears as an appendix to this volume.

Nearly everyone has commented on, and many have complained about, the length and girth of *PFG*. My book is branded as gigantic, enormous, exhaustive, sprawling, bloated, and overly ambitious. Reviewers speculate it to be twenty-five times larger than Paul's letters—possibly larger than the Bible itself—and akin to the U.S. Tax Code. They say that reading *PFG* is trying to tame a monster, and takes the proverbial ten thousand years of Amazing Grace. The book is even said to constitute its own planetary system. Nearly every reviewer chastises me with the comment that less might have been more. I understand these comments, though naturally I disagree with them.

Beyond the sheer size of the book, reviewers have also commented on my rhetoric. Some consider it to be overcooked, runaway, purple, and "High Table." Readers point out that I repeat myself. Some are wearied by the prose, finding it excessively "baggy." My so-called knock-about lecture-hall style, say some, results in caricature and grand generalisations. I am sometimes shrill; sometimes too hard on those whose readings I reject. I smack their hands. (Curiously, however, I am chided for both over- and under-engaging my critics.) My writing is said to be idiosyncratic and self-indulgent, and limited to an Anglophone scholarship. It seems to some that I have both a box for everything and a magic wand that solves all problems.

Happily, positive estimations equally abound. *PFG* has been called my *summa theologica*; an "individual" work (that is, it does not adhere to a particular school); my most compelling academic book to date; rich and expansive, a magnum opus; a publishing event; an enormous intellectual achievement; a landmark. My reading of Paul is considered original and complete. *PFG* is said to possess clarity of argument, inner coherence, and accessibility of style.

Responding to these reviews, not line by line but in outline, is the purpose of the present little book. Under threat of my publisher, I have kept the focus upon the issues under debate, rather than individual scholars or schools of thought. Thus, each chapter in what follows turns on a key debatable issue in Paul, a specific either/or, or sometimes several either/ors. Those who have ears will hear my critics and their specific criticisms on every single page that follows. The chapters of this book are steeped in and shaped by the reviews. This method of working is a way of trying to honour the contribution my reviewers have made, without descending to the small-scale point-scoring one meets in the correspondence columns of the weekly reviews like the *Times Literary Supplement* or the *New York Review of Books* ("if only Professor Snooks had read what I say on page 249, he could not have accused me of such-and-such a view," and so on).

The five chapters represent a response to the five most questioned elements in my book. In fact, nearly all the reviewers I have listed above have lingered on most or all of these points, even if there were other specific points of disagreement as well. The first chapter thus takes up the question of Paul's theological coherence, particularly the way in which his Jewish context, and the story about Israel he inherited, interacted with what he came to believe about Jesus, a christological story. Chapter 2 follows on by tackling the debate over the background, origin, and implications of Paul's Christology. The third chapter addresses the questions of covenant and cosmos, narrative and apocalyptic. Chapter 4 focuses on the debate over Paul's view of who constitutes the people of

God; this chapter also addresses the question of whether justification belongs to Paul's soteriology or to his ecclesiology, or somehow to both. The final chapter then traces debates about method, both Paul's and ours, as well as questions of discovery and presentation, again, both Paul's and ours.

As with all history, there is here a problem of scale and complexity. Many times in the last few decades I have received responses to books, articles, and conference papers in which my critics have warned that my attempts at broad summaries, my sketches of large pictures, have not taken sufficient account of the complex detail of the actual evidence. *PFG* is my response to this: there is the detail, lots of it, pressed down, shaken together, and running over. This has then generated the opposite problem: too much information. Thus the circle continues. The present little book is not so much a guide to *PFG*, though some might find it helpful in that role. Nor, of course, can it repeat the detailed display of evidence or the exegetical discussions. Its aim is to clarify particular points where people have been puzzled. If it succeeds in moving the debate forward out of misunderstandings I will be content.

Quotations from the New Testament are taken from my own translation, *The Kingdom New Testament* (in the UK, *The New Testament for Everyone*), published by HarperOne in San Francisco and SPCK in London in 2011. Quotations from the Old Testament are taken from the New Revised Standard Version. I have sometimes made minor adjustments, for instance in referring to the divine name, or in the references to Jesus as *Christos*, which I had sometimes translated "king" but which I have here normally rendered as "Messiah."

In expressing my gratitude to my many reviewers, I should also say how grateful I am to Dr. Carey C. Newman of Baylor University Press both for the idea of this book and for coming to Scotland to stand over me for a memorable week while I wrote it. He and his colleagues at Baylor have made this an easy and enjoyable task. I am also, as ever, grateful to Sam

Richardson, Philip Law, and their colleagues at SPCK for their work at the London end. If I say that I am dedicating this book to my reviewers, as seems only right, I hope they will not be offended by the honour. We are engaged in a common task.

N. T. Wright
St Mary's College, St Andrews
June 2015

1

Paul and the Messiah

Knowing the Name or Having the Mind?

"We have the mind of the Messiah." With this dramatic statement (1 Corinthians 2:16), Paul sums up his central aim and his central belief. His letters are designed to generate, sustain, and develop in their readers the art and capacity to *think Christianly*, that is, to think "in Christ," "in the Messiah." The phrase "Christian theology" was invented quite some time after Paul's day, but with hindsight we can say that he was already doing it—in the sense of "theology," not simply as a subject to be learned, but as a task to be undertaken. Behind all the debates as to whether he meant this or that, whether one framework of understanding or another enables us best to grasp his overall thrust and detailed meanings, there looms this larger project: that his hearers would become mature in their thinking (1 Corinthians 14:20), that they would be "transformed by the renewing of their minds" (Romans 12:2), that they would think in a particular way among themselves "with the mind that you have because you belong to the Messiah, Jesus" (Philippians 2:5). Paul could not possibly teach his little groups of converts everything he might have wanted to teach them, either in his short visits or his even shorter letters. But he wasn't trying to teach them everything. He was teaching them to think in such a way that they would be able to work things out for themselves. He wasn't interested simply in handing on to them true ideas and rules for living. He wanted them to *think messianically*, to think as Messiah-people. They would meet many new challenges, and they would need the mind of the Messiah if they were to meet these challenges with integrity and courage.

The reason there was to be a new way of thinking was because there was a new creation. A new mind for a new world:

> From this moment on, therefore, we don't regard anybody from a merely human point of view. Even if we once regarded the Messiah that way, we don't do so any longer. Thus, if anyone is in the Messiah, there is a new creation! Old things have gone, and look—everything has become new!
>
> (2 Corinthians 5:16-17)

The context of that statement was Paul's exposition of his own vocation, designed to explain himself to a congregation that had become suspicious of him. It seems that they were trying to measure him by the cultural expectations of the day, and he didn't match up. They wanted a success story, and he seemed to be always in trouble, always suffering. They wanted the kind of flashy "wisdom" they were used to hearing from the well-known teachers of the day, but Paul used a straight-talking "freedom of speech" which made them uncomfortable. They were trying to fit him and his message into their own culture, but he was insisting that he represented a new culture which was being born—and that they themselves, having already believed in Jesus the Messiah, were part of it.

This sense of a new world being born, catching people up into a new life within it, came from Paul's Jewish heritage. To understand that is to understand the heart of what Paul was about, and also the reason why he ran into trouble so often. The word "Messiah" itself, which comes out as the Greek term *Christos* in Paul's writings, was not simply a proper name. It meant "the anointed one," and Paul, like some other Jews of his day, linked it to passages in Israel's scriptures which spoke of a coming king through whom Israel's God, the world's creator, would not only rescue Israel itself but also bring new justice, harmony, and peace to the whole world. It was, we suppose, ancient prophecies like that, long mulled over, frequently sung in worship, that caused people to wonder whether this or that first-century figure was "the Messiah": several possible candidates came and went, their claims usually being disproved by a violent death. Some people wondered whether John the Baptist was the Messiah; he denied it, but in any case he, too, met a bloody end. As for Jesus of Nazareth, well, his followers really did believe that he was the Messiah; and this claim was publicly mocked, and visibly disproved, when the Roman governor had him executed with the phrase "King of the Jews" written above his head in three languages. So much for your "king."

Paul's belief in a new world being born was the direct result of the dramatic moment when he was confronted with Jesus himself, raised from the dead by Israel's God. Jesus' resurrection was, he believed, the launch of the new creation, a new world being born from the womb of the old. The resurrection of Jesus was the flash point, illuminating everything in all directions like a sudden bolt of lightning on a dark night. It gave Paul a new way of looking at the past, particularly at the long story of Israel and its hidden purpose. It gave him a new way of looking at the future, particularly the ultimate future of the whole cosmos coming to share this new creation. It gave him, not least, a new way of looking at himself, as he found himself swept along in this same moment, this movement, leaving behind one world and finding himself caught up in the new one.

All this comes to dramatic expression in Paul's most vivid little letter, the fiercely controversial epistle to the Galatians. This is not the moment for a full exposition, or even an explanation of why he deemed it necessary to write in this way. But let us at least consider how the letter starts and finishes, and what is meant by some of its central and dramatic claims. Here is Paul starting off, setting up the terms of the discussion:

> Grace to you and peace from God our father and Jesus the Messiah, our Lord, who gave himself for our sins, to rescue us from the present evil age, according to the will of God our father, to whom be glory to the ages of ages. Amen.

> (Galatians 1:3-5)

And here he is rounding it all off at the end:

> As for me, God forbid that I should boast—except in the cross of our Lord Jesus the Messiah, through whom the world has been crucified to me and I to the world. Circumcision, you see, is nothing; neither is uncircumcision! What matters is new creation. Peace and mercy on everyone who lines up by that standard—yes, on God's Israel.

> (Galatians 6:14-16)

What matters is new creation. Something had happened through which the world was a different place, circumcised Israel and uncircumcised non-Jews were different people, and Paul himself was a different person. He uses his own example to drive home the point after reflecting on a moment when the dramatic newness of his message had been under severe threat:

> Through the law I died to the law, so that I might live to God. I have been crucified with the Messiah. I am, however, alive—but it isn't me any longer; it's the Messiah who lives in me. And the life I do still live in the flesh, I live

within the faithfulness of the son of God, who loved me
and gave himself for me.

(Galatians 2:19-20)

Look, he was saying, everything has become new. This, for
Paul, was the defining, Messiah-shaped truth not simply
about the world in general, or about this or that individual in
particular, but about the community that found itself formed
by the new energy which pulsated through what Paul called
"the gospel," the good-news message he announced. Declaring
that the Jesus who had been executed by the Romans was the
true Messiah of Israel and hence the true Lord of the world
carried power, and hence also danger. People of all sorts found
themselves grasped and transformed by this message, indeed
(they would say) by this Lord. The result was a community
significantly different from anything previously known:

> You see, every one of you who has been baptised into the
> Messiah has put on the Messiah. There is no longer Jew
> or Greek; there is no longer slave or free; there is no "male
> and female"; you are all one in the Messiah, Jesus. And, if
> you belong to the Messiah, you are Abraham's family. You
> stand to inherit the promises.

(Galatians 3:27-29)

We will come back later on to the question of Abraham,
his family, and his inheritance. But here, at the heart of one
of Paul's sharpest and perhaps earliest letters, we find what
this "new creation" means in practice. It means a new family, a
new people. When we examine Paul's letters, long and short,
sad and happy, vivacious one minute and meditative the next,
we find that he keeps coming back to this family, this strange
new assemblage of people, thrown together against the grain
of social customs or cultural expectations. The Messiah could
not have two or more families; there was only the one, formed

by, and as witness to, the extraordinary act of new creation which had come about in and through Jesus and his death and resurrection. This was not a "new religion." Paul believed it was the start of a new world.

Paul's letters are urging two things in particular on this family. They are to work out in practice what it means to be united: Paul knew very well that this was a hard task, needing constant pastoral work and exhortation. If this startling ideal was to come anywhere near reality, a disparate collection of people, finding themselves part of this new-creation movement with others who would not be their natural friends or associates, needed to call on fresh reserves of humility, sympathy, and above all the virtue which Paul made central, *agapē*, "love." This, indeed, is near the heart of what he means by having the Messiah's mind:

> Here's how to do it. Hold on to the same love; bring your innermost lives into harmony; fix your minds on the same object. Never act out of selfish ambition or vanity; instead, regard everybody else as your superior. Look after each other's best interests, not your own. *This is how you should think among yourselves—with the mind that you have because you belong to the Messiah, Jesus.* . . .

> (Philippians 2:2-5)

The second thing goes very closely with this. The people who, to their own surprise, are called into being through the news about Jesus are to discover *the new way of being human,* the way through which the creator's original intention was to be lived out. Shortly after the passage just quoted, Paul insists on this:

> There must be no grumbling and disputing in anything you do. That way, nobody will be able to fault you, and you'll be pure and spotless children of God in the middle of

a twisted and depraved generation. You are to shine among them like lights in the world, clinging to the word of life.

(Philippians 2:14-16)

To make this point, which as we can see joins up easily with his emphasis on "unity," Paul speaks of the old humanity in terms of "flesh," which for him means the decaying, corruptible old world and its way of life, and of the new humanity in terms of the dynamic power which has been unleashed through the gospel, the "spirit":

Live by the spirit, and you won't do what the flesh wants you to. . . . Now the works of the flesh are obvious. They are such things as fornication, uncleanness, licentiousness, idolatry, sorcery, hostilities, strife, jealousy, bursts of rage, selfish ambition, factiousness, divisions, moods of envy, drunkenness, wild partying, and similar things. . . . But the fruit of the spirit is love, joy, peace, great-heartedness, kindness, generosity, faithfulness, gentleness, self-control.

(Galatians 5:16, 19-21, 22-23)

At a more formal level, Paul can sum up this sense of the life of "new creation" as "holiness." This, he says, is the divine gift which comes through belonging to the Messiah, to having "died with him" and been "raised with him," as we already saw in Galatians:

The Messiah, having been raised from the dead, will never die again. Death no longer has any authority over him. . . . In the same way you, too, must calculate yourselves as being dead to sin, and alive to God in the Messiah, Jesus.

(Romans 6:9-11)

That "calculation" is yet another aspect for Paul of having the Messiah's mind. And it goes on:

So don't allow sin to rule in your mortal body, to make you
obey its desires. Nor should you present your limbs and
organs to sin to be used for its wicked purposes. Rather,
present yourselves to God, as people alive from the dead,
and your limbs and organs to God, to be used for the righ-
teous purposes of his covenant. Sin won't actually rule over
you, you see, since you are not under law but under grace.

(Romans 6:12-14)

It's all part of the same thing. Having the Messiah's mind
means learning how to live in the new way. Romans 6, from
which this passage is taken, depends on Romans 5, where
Paul explicitly contrasts the old kind of humanity and the new
kind. Adam and the Messiah are the two types of humanity,
and the point about messianic humanness is that it has come
through death, thereby stripping off all the signs of corruption
and decay, and has come up into a new life, the life the creator
always intended.

For Paul, then, the "good-news" announcement that the
crucified Jesus of Nazareth had been raised from the dead
generated a surprised new community, the community of
Messiah-people who were to see themselves as a single family,
working at maintaining that unity, and working, too, at the
difficult task of "holiness." And for this they needed the Messiah's mind.

Before we explore this further, and look at what we can
loosely and with hindsight call Paul's model of "Christian theology," there are two other things to notice. People who study
human societies, ancient and modern, often comment on the
fact that all social groups, large and small, have certain practices which mark them out, certain "rituals" (whether they call
them that or not) which sum up "who we are." All social groups
also have an implicit story by which they live. We in the modern western world often fail to recognise our own controlling
narratives, but they are there all right, once you know where to

look, visible in every newspaper, advertisement, chat show. We can see this sort of thing more easily, perhaps, in other people's worlds, just as we notice our neighbour's wallpaper more than we notice our own.

With Paul, we can see that certain actions marked out his communities, and gave them a particular focus. Baptism and the Lord's Supper were focused on Jesus, and on his death and resurrection. These actions constituted his followers as Messiah-people, as having themselves died and been raised, and as belonging to a new social as well as theological entity. It was no doubt hard for them to make that new society a reality, just as it was no doubt hard to grasp Paul's teaching about the sudden new creation.

One of the ways of making it easier, perhaps, was the story. Paul frequently alludes to the larger story of Israel, well known in his world through the scriptures, less well known but still important in the non-Jewish world. We have already mentioned Abraham, and at certain significant points Paul lines up the new community as, no doubt to their surprise, the single family which God promised to the patriarch. One of the other great moments in Israel's story was the Exodus, the time when God rescued his people from slavery, gave them the Law, came to dwell with them in the Tabernacle, and led them to the inheritance he had promised them. Paul draws on this story in several different ways, and if we ponder for a moment we can see why: it was common knowledge among the early Jesus-followers that Jesus himself had gone up to Jerusalem at Passover-time, Exodus-time, and that his crucifixion and resurrection were irrevocably coloured by that setting. What we see in Paul, fleshing out his idea of *new creation*, is *new Exodus*; and this is the story that, in his retellings of it, helps his communities to see themselves as called to unity and holiness. The dramatic, unexpected event of Jesus' resurrection compelled Paul to revisit his entire world of story, symbol, practice, and

thought, and to see it with new-creation eyes. That seeing is
what he refers to as "the mind of the Messiah."

So when we come to consider what is sometimes called
"Paul's theology," we are not investigating a philosophical
system detached from reality. Much western thought in the
modern period has assumed that what really matters is a
set of ideas which can be lined up, integrated, and held as a
unity in the mind. Paul, to be sure, has a subtle and sophisticated set of ideas, but they do not exist for their own sake.
They exist because *only by clinging on to something like this set
of ideas will the community have any chance of being united and
holy.* What we call "Paul's theology" has a particular purpose:
to sustain, direct, and energise the lives of the little Messiah-
communities that have come into existence through his good-
news announcement (and, in one or two cases, a community
which he had not himself founded). The argument I have made
in my longer work on Paul can be summarised as follows: that
Paul invented something which with hindsight can be called
"Christian theology" because only by giving themselves to this
task—learning to think Christianly about God, about God's
people, and God's future—can the church be sustained and
energised in unity and holiness.

This is so particularly because, as Paul constantly reminded
his hearers, the good-news announcement was always going to
mean trouble. Suffering would come to those who found themselves caught up in it. They were at the leading edge of new creation, and the old creation would resent it and fight back. He
warned them of this, he reminded them that his own sufferings were part of the same struggle, and he interpreted these
sufferings too as part of Messiah-living. There is, to be sure, a
sense in which the Messiah's sufferings, centred on his crucifixion, were unique. He did something one-off which would
never need to be done again. But for Paul, as for other early
Christian writers like the authors of 1 Peter and Revelation,
there is also a sense in which Jesus' sufferings set the pattern

which Messiah-followers should expect to see worked out in their own lives. This is why they need, not merely to grit their teeth and see it through—Paul is not a Stoic, despite many parallels between that great movement and his thought!—but to *understand* what it means to be new-creation people. And to understand this they must learn how to think about God, God's people, and God's future.

"Learning to think about God" is all very well. But if it really is the true God one is thinking about, one cannot just think; one must pray. "Thinking about God" in the abstract, as though "God" were an object we might discuss dispassionately, makes about as much sense as "thinking about seismology" in a cool, detached way while in the middle of a major earthquake. How you pray, and to whom you pray, are therefore organically related. Some of Paul's most profound theological insights are expressed in the form of prayers.

These are essentially Jewish prayers, but they are Jewish prayers with a difference; because Paul's thinking, his theology, is Jewish thinking, but it is Jewish thinking with a difference. For him, having the Messiah's mind meant bringing a whole world of Jewish thinking into a new focus, a new frame, because the Messiah himself, so Paul believed, had brought the whole life of God's ancient people into a new focus, a new frame. The Messiah was the catalyst for Paul's rethought theology, just as he was the intimate focus of Paul's reconceived life of prayer. For many years people who have written about Paul have struggled with the question, Was Paul basically a Jewish or a non-Jewish thinker? The question is far more complicated than has often been imagined, but if we are forced into this either/or, the answer is clear: Paul was a Jewish thinker, and remained a Jewish thinker.

But two things had happened which make the proposal that he was a non-Jewish thinker at least comprehensible. First, he believed that Israel's Messiah had been crucified, and that this was not simply a strange, dark accident, a blip in the divine purposes, but that it was indicative of, and centrally instrumental in, the purpose that Israel's God had had in mind all along. Some of Paul's most difficult and profound writing comes when he is wrestling with this question. Second, he believed, in line with many scriptural prophecies, that if and when Israel's Messiah showed up, he would be the ruler of the nations. Put those two together, and you have the signposts which some have misread as saying, There we are, Paul was really a gentile thinker, a representative of something called "gentile Christianity" as opposed to "Jewish Christianity," someone who abandoned his Jewish heritage and put together a scheme of thought from bits and pieces of the surrounding non-Jewish world. That, I am convinced, is a deep and damaging mistake. Paul was articulating and working out *a Jewish message for the non-Jewish world*, even as he was articulating *a messianic critique of the Jewish world* of his day. We should not be surprised that his own contemporaries found this difficult and controversial, and that the controversies have rumbled on into our own day.

What, then, are the contours of Paul's "theology," this Messiah-based, prayer-shaped fresh articulation of Jewish belief? The answer is that they grow out of the shocking new event, the messianic event of Jesus' death and resurrection, and the consequent gift of the Spirit; and that event precipitates a fresh, strong, and supple rereading of the central categories of Jewish thought. Paul redraws these around the Messiah—and also around the Spirit, since for Paul his own work, the effectiveness of the good-news announcement, and the ongoing work of transformation in the lives of believers were all unthinkable except as the outworking of a new divine energy, unleashed through the messianic events.

When we speak of "central categories" of Jewish thought, however, we are confronted with a problem: Jews did not, and still do not, habitually articulate their central thoughts about their God, their identity as a people, and their future hopes in terms of a system. Generalisations are of course dangerous, but Jews have always preferred to tell stories: small stories in which some nugget of wisdom suddenly glints at us out of the dark, larger stories in which the strange purposes of the One God emerge like mountains out of a mist. But within the stories, and the meaning that emerges through them, there are indeed certain great truths around which some Jewish thinkers have organised everything else. We have already mentioned them two or three times, but it is time to put labels on to them: monotheism, election, and eschatology. One God; one people of God; one future for God's world. These, I suggest, are the central pillars of Paul's thought, each redesigned (but not, he would insist, abandoned) around Messiah and Spirit. This is what Paul wants his readers to grapple with. "Theology," for him and for them, is not simply a set of theories to be learned, but a task to be undertaken, a task for each generation, each church, each reader. It is by struggling with these great truths, in the midst of suffering and bewilderment (of which Paul himself had more than his fair share), in the light of fresh readings of scripture (to which Paul himself gave massive impetus), in the context of a new kind of prayer (which Paul insisted on as the constant setting), that the communities he founded would become what they were designed to be. This is what it meant to work at "the mind of the Messiah," to think in the new ways appropriate within the new creation.

For Paul this is all the more important since the messianic and revelatory events of cross and resurrection meant that the symbolic world within which he had formerly lived had been transformed from top to bottom. If the one God had launched his new creation, thereby summoning into being a new people no longer from one nation but from the whole world, the symbolic markers by which the Jewish people had been defined over against the rest of the world were no longer relevant, and to cling to them or rebuild them would be to indicate that the new creation had not after all begun. (That is part of the central message of Galatians.) What, then, would mark out this new people, this multi-ethnic conglomeration of messianic folk? For Paul, the answer was: *this reworked belief.* That is one of the reasons why the only badge he will acknowledge as marking out the new "family" is what he calls *pistis,* "faith" or "faithfulness," "loyalty" or "belief." For Paul, *pistis* is all of that and more. What he means by "faith" has deep roots in Israel's scriptures, but the new circumstances of the new people mean that for Paul it assumes a central position it did not have before. (Some older writers, seeing the way the concept of "faith" had developed in some Christian theology, supposed that there were "two types of faith," the distinctively Jewish and distinctively Christian types, but to read Paul like this is a mistake. The point is that "faith," in its rich biblical senses, assumed a significance never before imagined.) For Paul, *pistis* is the personal allegiance to the God who was now to be known as "the God who raised Jesus from the dead"; personal confession that "Jesus is Lord." The reason Paul articulates what we later call "theology," and the reason that ever afterwards the followers of Jesus have "done theology" while other great movements have not, or not in the same way, is that for Paul the fresh revelation, the unveiling-in-action of the One God, demands nothing less. This task, this prayerful and scriptural reflection on who God is, who God's people are, what God's purposes are for the world—this is part of the characteristic praxis of the Messiah-people. This marks them out.

Now is not the moment to explore again the three great categories of Paul's thought, but we may at least say three things. First, Paul's theological vision grows directly out of his belief that the God who made the world had raised Jesus from the dead. This was a new moment. From all that we know of the Pharisees, we can be sure that Saul of Tarsus had believed that when Israel's God finally did what he had promised to do, he would raise from the dead all his people, possibly even all the human race. This would be part of his great final act of putting everything right, the moment for which, in the Psalms and the prophets, all creation and especially all Israel had been waiting. Paul's new-found belief that the crucified Jesus had been raised from the dead meant, therefore, that *God had done in the middle of history, to one person, what he was expected to do at the end of history, to all his people.* Central to Paul's whole thought was this essentially *eschatological* belief: that a new time had dawned, the "now" time, the "messianic" time. Old things had passed away; the new had arrived—but it had arrived in the middle of the "old" time which was still lumbering along on the road of corruption that led to death. Right from the start, therefore, we are dealing with a radically new moment, a new divine action, which compelled Paul—Saul of Tarsus as he then was—to see everything differently.

Second, however, the "everything" which he was seeing differently was, demonstrably in passage after passage, the "everything" which we know from the Jewish scriptures and subsequent literature to have been common coin among Paul's contemporaries. Granted, there were some favourite texts in the Jewish world which he did not use. Granted, as he thought back through his scriptures he highlighted some themes in ways which before he would not have done; we have just seen that "faith" is a good example of this. But there is a constant and regular family likeness between what he was doing and what other Jews of roughly the same period were doing as they, like him, struggled to make sense of the divine promises and purposes and the strange ways they both were and were not working out as anticipated. We must never say, therefore, that when Paul was speaking of the Jewish world he said, thought, or implied that there was something "wrong" with that world, with its practices, its stories, or its beliefs. That has been the shadow side of so much writing about Paul, but it is based on a mistake. The mistake is to imagine that Paul was offering a new sort of "religion," and that he contrasted it, measuring both against some kind of abstract standard, with a "religion" which we can call "Judaism." (The one time he speaks of "Judaism," in Galatians 1:13-14, it does not refer to what we think as "the religion called Judaism," but to the *activity* of zealously propagating a particular way of life.) On the contrary: some of the sharpest things he says by way of critique against the position he had formerly occupied, that of persecuting the followers of Jesus, he takes from the scriptures themselves, the scriptures which (like Deuteronomy 32) had always warned that "Israel" would wander away from God's path and that God would do new things to make them jealous, the scriptures which (like Isaiah 52 or Ezekiel 36) spoke of the nations of the world looking at Israel and blaspheming Israel's God rather than praising him. When Paul sums up the purpose of his mission in Romans 15, insisting once more on the unity of the Messiah's people and on their worship of the one God, he sees this, for all its sudden strangeness and radical newness, not as a fresh idea but as the reality to which scripture had pointed all along:

> Welcome one another, therefore, as the Messiah has welcomed you, to God's glory. Let me tell you why: the Messiah became a servant of the circumcised people in order to demonstrate the truthfulness of God—that is, to confirm the promises to the patriarchs, and to bring the nations to praise God for his mercy. As the Bible says:

> > *That is why I will praise you among the nations,*
> > *And will sing to your name.*

> And again it says,

> > *Rejoice, you nations, with his people.*

> And again,

Praise the Lord, all nations,
And let all the peoples sing his praise.

And Isaiah says once more:

There shall be the root of Jesse,
The one who rises up to rule the nations;
The nations shall hope in him.

(Romans 15:7-12, quoting from Psalm 18:49,
Deuteronomy 32:43, Psalm 117:1,
and Isaiah 11:10)

Third, Paul's self-description was not simply that he was a Messiah-person, someone who lived "in the Messiah" and claimed to have "the Messiah's mind." He was also "the apostle to the gentiles," the one chosen to bring this essentially Jewish message to the non-Jewish world. Most of his readers (not all) were from that world, the world of a long Hellenistic culture replete with its own varied philosophical, religious, and political history. All the places where Paul focused his work were also part of the newly burnished Roman empire. Rome had had an empire for many years, but only in the generation before Paul had it had an emperor as such, being ruled before by a string of leaders, elected annually, in a system designed to stop any one man becoming too powerful. The system had eventually imploded with the assassination of Julius Caesar and the civil wars that followed, from which Octavian, Caesar's heir, emerged as the last man standing, declaring that he had brought peace and justice to the world, bringing about a new golden age. This was the world to which Paul went with the very Jewish message about the one God, reworked around the Messiah Jesus, and with his founding of communities giving allegiance to Jesus as "lord." For Paul, the golden age—not that he called it that—had come about through the death and resurrection of Jesus, not with the accession of this or that pagan world ruler. For Paul, in fact—and this was central to all he thought and did—the death and resurrection of Jesus were the events in which, in a concentrated moment of sovereign divine power, the "powers" of the world, both visible and invisible, had been decisively defeated. Something happened with the crucifixion of Jesus which meant that the dark "powers" that dragged the world down into corruption and death had been defeated. That victory was signaled precisely by Jesus' resurrection, demonstrating that death itself no longer had ultimate power. For Paul, the resurrection of the crucified Jesus formed the heart of a new philosophy which could take on the world and reshape its categories. For Paul, the resurrection of Jesus and his installation as "lord" formed the heart of a new politics in which communities came into being that modeled a new kind of human existence. Whatever we say and think about Paul, we must remember that as the "apostle to the gentiles" he saw the non-Jewish world as his primary audience, and his apostleship to that world as his primary task. His very Jewish theology was not primarily designed to outflank the Jewish world that had rejected the message of Jesus and the message about Jesus. It was designed, in a very Jewish fashion, to confront the powers of the world, and the thought-forms which expressed their way of life, with the news of new creation. Learning to have the Messiah's mind meant learning to out-think the *pagan* world with the news of a new way of living.

The message of new creation was not, after all, a message about a private world, hidden away from the present public one. That would be the high road to a kind of Gnosticism, a world of secret enlightenment in which the initiates would effectively be cut off from the rest of the world. That might have been easier; certainly it would have been less confrontational. For Paul, this was not an option. The sovereign divine act which was concentrated in the death and resurrection of the Messiah, and the sovereign divine act which continued through the good-news announcement in the power of the Spirit, meant that new creation had been launched *in the middle of the old one.* Those who were caught up in it were new-creation people. Their thought-forms were the radically new versions of previous enquiry. Their story was the radically new version of the ancient story of Israel. Their God was the radically reunderstood, the freshly invoked, God of Israel, now revealed in shocking suddenness as the Father of Jesus the Messiah. These are the parameters within which Paul reworked his Jewish theology as the Messiah-mind that would hold together the followers of Jesus and enable them to live as God's holy people, in and through the suffering they would undoubtedly experience. This is the way he taught them to pray. This is how he taught them to read the scriptures. This was how they were to be "transformed by the renewing of their minds."

As we look back, then, we find the basic solution to one of the debates about Paul which has rumbled on over the last two centuries:

a. Was Paul simply a Jewish thinker who happened to know the name of the Messiah?

This idea has been proposed in various ways, but it does not seem to catch the radical newness of Paul's message. Or,

b. Was Paul, then, a Hellenistic thinker who constructed a non-Jewish scheme of thought in which fragments from his Jewish world remain but without influencing the real structure?

This, too, has been tried, both by thinkers who wanted to praise Paul for breaking free from Judaism and by others who wanted to attack him for the same reason. But it will not do.

c. Was Paul, then, a Jewish thinker whose thought had been radically renewed from within by a new event which meant what it meant for him within a Jewish and particularly scriptural frame of reference?

Paul would have said, Yes. Israel's Messiah, interpreted by Israel's scriptures, was the heart of his thought. His death and resurrection meant that everything would now be seen in a different, though still radically Jewish, light. Everything: including even Israel's God.

2

How to Begin with Jesus

What Did Paul Know, and How Did He Come to Know It?

Paul talks about Jesus a lot. That is putting it mildly. Almost everything he says either starts with Jesus or comes back to him. He sees himself as defined by Jesus, as a man "in the Messiah." The pattern of Jesus' death and resurrection is stitched into his consciousness to the extent that even when he is talking about sex or money, food or slavery, let alone the larger issues of judgment and mercy, unity, and holiness— whatever he touches, he relates it to Jesus.

So what did Paul think about Jesus? Who did he think he was? What did he think he had achieved? And—of enormous importance in recent discussions—how did Paul come to these conclusions? What drove him in this direction?

Here we can set up the two questions of this chapter as follows:

a. Did Paul have a robust belief about Jesus, including identifying him in some sense with the God of Israel, or are beliefs like that only to be found later in early Christianity, after Paul's day?

b. Was Paul's belief about Jesus a fresh flowering of already existent Jewish material, or is there some other signal means by which he developed his mature views?

The first question is now less controversial than it was a generation ago, but it still demands careful enquiry. It seems to me now beyond reasonable doubt that when Paul was speaking about Jesus, not least when he seems to be quoting poems or prayers in which Jesus figures prominently, he places Jesus not only *alongside* the one God of Israel but somehow *within* the identity of Israel's God. Paul clearly sees himself as a Jewish-style monotheist; that is to say, he believes in the One God as creator of a world which, though spoiled and corrupt, remains the good creation of this good God. There were non-Jewish monotheists at the time, some of whom believed that all the various pagan divinities were simply different ways of speaking about one divine essence lying behind them all. That is not Paul's position. For him, the one God remains radically distinct from the world, though also intimately involved with it. And, as a sure sign of this Jewish position, what Paul says about food and drink, marriage and sex, and also about the divine judgment through which the one God will be "all in all," fits like a glove with the ancient Jewish belief, rooted in scripture.

There is no suggestion, then, that if Paul did believe that Jesus somehow shared the "identity" of God, this meant he was adding Jesus to a potential pantheon. If he says things which sound as though he is thinking of Jesus as in some sense "divine," he does not intend this as a compromise of Jewish monotheism.

In fact, we find some of the clearest pieces of evidence *within explicitly monotheistic contexts*. The argument of 1 Corinthians 8, 9, and 10, dealing in detail with the critical and tricky problems posed for Messiah-believers by the question of whether or not one should eat food that had been sacrificed to an idol, is answered fundamentally by Jewish monotheism:

idols don't really exist, there is no god but One, the earth
belongs to him along with everything in it (1 Corinthians
8:1-4; 10:26). Paul quotes major Jewish monotheistic texts to
this effect: Psalm 24 at the end of the argument, Deuteronomy 6 at the start.

*But in both cases he discovers Jesus within the monotheistic
text.* Deuteronomy 6:4, a basic "confession of faith" which contains a strong implicit warning against idolatry, says "YHWH is
our God, YHWH alone." Actually, that English translation is
controversial; the dense Hebrew phrase YHWH *eloheynu* YHWH
ehad could mean "YHWH is our God, YHWH alone" or perhaps
"YHWH our God, YHWH is One." Other translations are also
suggested, but they do not affect the key point. In Paul's Greek
Bible the divine name YHWH is translated *kyrios*, "the Lord,"
corresponding to the regular reverent substitution, in reading
aloud, of the Hebrew *adonai*, "my Lord," for the name itself.
The Greek version of the passage in question thus reads, *kyrios
ho theos hēmōn, kyrios heis estin* (the Lord our God, the Lord
is one). In several other well-known passages Paul quotes lines
from the Greek Bible in which *kyrios* originally stands for the
divine name, but seems clearly to be referring to Jesus. So it is
here, quite explicitly:

> But for us
> There is one God, the father,
> From whom are all things, and we live to him and
>   for him;
> And one Lord, Jesus the Messiah,
> Through whom are all things, and we live
>   through him.

> (1 Corinthians 8:6)

The basic Greek here is very close to that of Deuteronomy,
which means that the explanatory additions stand out even
more sharply: One God . . . one Lord . . . is developed so that
"God" is made to stand for "the father," and "Lord" for "Jesus

the Messiah." Paul has expanded the original formula, adding in both halves the phrase "all things," which emphasises the point he wants to make throughout chapters 8, 9, and 10: the whole creation belongs to the One God, One Lord, so when we think about idols, their temples, and food that has been offered to them, one should never suppose that the idols now "own" things which are in fact part of the good creation.

In fact, the whole argument Paul is mounting at this point depends on what we might call the *christological redefinition of Jewish monotheism*. The Jewish monotheism is the basis: that, Paul insists, is where Messiah-people stand. That is how they know where they are in relation to idols and their shrines. But in case anyone should suppose that, because as monotheists they know that idols are non-existent, they can eat idol-meat without a further thought, he insists on the christological focus: to behave like that might cause the ruin of "someone with a weak conscience," who might be betrayed into actual idolatry by seeing a fellow Messiah-follower eating sacrificial meat. This, Paul says, would be sinning not just against the one God, but against the Messiah (1 Corinthians 8:11-12).

There are many other passages which make the same point. The best-known other relevant passage is undoubtedly Philippians 2:6-11, often seen as an early hymn or poem which Paul here quotes as the centrepiece of his argument for the unity (2:1-4) and holiness (2:12-16) of the church. If the aim is to teach people to think with "the mind of the Messiah," then the Messiah's own decisions and actions are what matter. Here is the famous "poem":

> Who, though in God's form, did not
> Regard his equality with God
> As something he ought to exploit.
>
> Instead, he emptied himself,
> And received the form of a slave,
> Being born in the likeness of humans.

And then, having human appearance,
He humbled himself, and became
Obedient even to death,

Yes, even the death of the cross.

And so God has greatly exalted him,
And to him in his favour has given
The name which is over all names:

That now at the name of Jesus
Every knee within heaven shall bow—
On earth, too, and under the earth;

And every tongue shall confess
That Jesus, Messiah, is Lord
To the glory of God, the father.

(Philippians 2:6-11)

Whole books have been written on this poem alone, and rightly so. It is one of the most extraordinary pieces of early Christian writing, and tells us something important which is worth pondering. It looks, from this passage and others (I am thinking, for instance, of Colossians 1:15-20 and indeed John 1:1-18) as though some of the most profound ideas about the identity of Jesus were first formulated in poetry and only later translated into (as it were) abstract categories.

There is another fascinating point which emerges from this and related passages. It has often been assumed that, if Paul did have a "high" view of Jesus, this must have been controversial; that it might even be one of the contributory reasons why the young Saul of Tarsus persecuted the early church, and why he in turn was persecuted when he embraced this faith. There is no evidence for any of this. Paul speaks in this way of Jesus in order to make other points. There is no sign that he is consciously innovating, or telling his readers something they do not already know. If there are controversial things in the passages in question, they are in the implications of this view of Jesus, not in the view itself.

Anyway, the main point for our purposes to emerge from this passage is at the beginning and end of the poem. In the first stanza, it is clear that in Paul's eyes Jesus, prior to his human birth, already possessed "equality with God." Paul has often been taken to say either that he did not possess that equality and that he did not grasp at it, or that he did possess it but did not cling on to it. Neither is true either to the Greek idiom he is using or to the logic of the poem as a whole. The point of the entire poem is that, at the end, Jesus the Messiah is hailed as *kyrios*, with every knee bowing before him. The reason for this (flagged up with the "and so" as the poem turns the corner after the single line in the middle) is that he has done what only God can do. His humble death, the death of the cross, the slave's death, has somehow accomplished what God himself had promised to achieve.

This already looks ahead to the next part of our investigation, but we need to notice how this crucial point is made. As Paul echoes Deuteronomy 6 in 1 Corinthians 8, taking one of the most obviously "monotheistic" passages from Israel's scriptures and finding Jesus in the middle of it, so here he does something very similar with Isaiah 45. The prophetic passage is a scornful denunciation of all pagan idols. There is, after all, only one God, Israel's God, the creator of the whole world:

> Turn to me and be saved, all the ends of the earth!
>> For I am God, and there is no other.
> By myself I have sworn,
>> from my mouth has gone forth in righteousness
>> a word that shall not return:
> To me every knee shall bow,
>> every tongue shall swear.
> Only in YHWH, it shall be said of me,
>> are righteousness and strength;

> All who were incensed against him
> shall come to him and be ashamed.
> In YHWH all the offspring of Israel
> shall triumph and glory.

(Isaiah 45:22-25)

The one God declares that to him alone every knee shall bow; only to him will every tongue swear allegiance. Paul declares that the honour which the one God will not share with anyone else he has shared with Jesus. And this christologically mono-theistic vision is in the direct service of the "messianic mind" he wants his congregations to grasp, so that they may learn the secret of a united and holy common life.

These arguments have been sufficiently rehearsed else-where, and this is merely a brief summary of two of the key pieces of evidence. The first question is I think answered. Paul did indeed hold a view of Jesus in which he was identified, somehow or other, with Israel's God. But this leads to the much harder question: how did Paul come to this view? How did the "high Christology" of our earliest sources develop so quickly and thoroughly that it seems to have become accepted and uncontroversial within the first decades of the movement?

Here the two views have historically looked like this. First, there is the older denial: a high Christology is so un-Jewish that it must have been built up on the basis of non-Jewish ele-ments culled from pagan philosophy or religion. Either Paul was thinking of the "*kyrios*"-cults of the ancient world, or he was wanting to take a title that had been applied to Caesar and apply it instead to Jesus, or something else down that line.

Why was this view adopted, and why did it become so popular? Here is an important note: this older denial, this insistence that a high Christology must be non-Jewish, was eagerly put about by two quite different groups. First, it was the accepted view of those historians of religion who, follow-ing F. C. Baur, postulated two radically different movements in the early church. They guessed at a "Jewish Christian" movement and a "gentile Christian" one, the latter breaking away from "Judaism" and inventing a different sort of religion, a different sort of theology—including a "high Christology." Second, the great majority of Jewish writers about early Christianity affirmed, and many such still affirm, that since Jews are monotheists it would be impossible for them to embrace anything like this "high Christology," so that we would have to say that Paul and others, insofar as they did embrace such a thing, were taking a very large step away from a Jewish position. Sometimes this point is made with a glance, or more than a glance, at the old problem of "Jesus and Paul": Paul, it is said, ascribed to Jesus these non-Jewish ideas which Jesus himself would either not have understood or would have been horrified to hear. Some who have been neither orthodox Christians nor orthodox Jews have seized on this argument eagerly to suggest that the heart of what became "Christianity" was based on a mistake which would have horrified the Founder himself.

The first historic view, then, is that high Christology is a late invention, without Jewish antecedents, drawing on non-Jewish (i.e., "pagan") sources. The second view, which has been making its way in leaps and bounds over the last generation, is the one I glanced at a moment ago: that Paul in fact places Jesus within the identity of Israel's God, using specifically monotheistic passages to mount specifically monotheistic arguments and discovering Jesus at the heart of it all. How in the world did Paul, or the Christian groups that existed even before he joined the movement, arrive so quickly at this view?

There are three kinds of answer to this question. Each offers an insufficient but necessary part of the ultimately sufficient condition for the evidence we have. First, one could say that Israel's scriptures always taught the coming of a "divine Messiah" who would die for the sins of the world and rise again; so that the first Christians simply fitted Jesus into an outline which was there already. Some older writers said this kind of thing, but such a view would not be widely adopted today.

Second, many have said that in the post-biblical Jewish literature we can see signs that Jews were already saying things about "intermediary figures," including some of the patriarchs (Abraham, Enoch), some abstract personified entities (Wisdom), and even some angels—things which, in the writings in question, made it sound as though these figures were being regarded as in some sense "divine." Such Jewish speculations about powerful "God-like" figures formed a larger matrix of thought. The early Christian experience of worship, in which the presence of Jesus was so strong, and corresponded so closely to Jewish ideas of the presence of Israel's One God, then made it not only natural but inevitable to see Jesus and the One God as somehow linked together in a dyadic structure in ways which emerge in Paul and elsewhere. This became one of the central distinguishing features of early Christianity. Fascinatingly, at least one variation on this view has been vigorously expounded by a leading Jewish scholar, thus reversing the argument of many generations: instead of "high Christology, therefore non-Jewish," we have, "all the key things about early Christianity were there in Judaism already"; instead of "everything you did, we rejected," "everything you did, we did first."

Third, we could say that it was the resurrection itself that convinced Paul and the others of Jesus' "divinity." This too has often been affirmed; indeed, it forms part of an older apologetic armoury: he was raised, therefore he was the son of God! Sometimes people have quoted Romans 1:3-4 to this effect: he was "marked out powerfully as God's son . . . by the resurrection of the dead." Often this has been stated as part of an older anti-Deist apologetic: the miracle proves his divinity! This ignores the fact that in Israel's scriptures all sorts of people perform remarkable works. One thinks of Elijah raising the dead. That doesn't suggest that we should predicate "divinity" either of Elijah himself or of the boy he resuscitates.

I think all of these suggestions are partly right, pointing in more or less the right direction, but that none by itself is sufficient. Even the combination of these three leaves unsaid what to me is most important. First, however, we need to say as clearly as possible that for Paul everything that mattered about Jesus was explosively unveiled in the combination of his death and resurrection. Saul of Tarsus was certainly not going about supposing that a dying-and-rising Messiah was on the way, only waiting for evidence that Jesus (who had been crucified as a messianic pretender) had been raised from the dead before declaring him to be Messiah and Lord, and in the full sense "son of God." But nor can the resurrection be seen in a vacuum. Even to a well-taught first-century Jew, the rising from the dead of one man, as an isolated event, would be a serious puzzle. It would mean that the world was a very odd place. This was not what was expected.

For that reason we do well to look for a combination of reasons, a confluence of events, ideas, and beliefs, none of which might be sufficient in itself to generate the evidence we have, but all of which, taken together, might just do so. And this is where I need to bring in the fourth possibility, which I think worked very closely with those just mentioned, the first and third in particular. It seems clear to me that neither Saul of Tarsus nor any other first-century Jew known to us was expecting what we might call an "incarnate Messiah," a Messiah who would be the living embodiment of Israel's God. (There are questions that could be raised here about the second-century leader Simeon ben Kosiba, the would-be "Messiah" of the 130s, and about what Rabbi Akiba may or may not have said or thought about him; but these must be put aside just now.)

But what many Jews manifestly expected, because it was there in their scriptures, especially the Psalms and prophets, and was picked up again and again in the evidence we have from the Second-Temple period, is that *Israel's God himself would act to deliver his people from the powers of evil and to set up his kingdom over the nations.* I think we have been looking for the wrong sort of evidence and hence in the wrong sort of place. I do not think Paul (or the other early Christians) were prepared for Jesus' resurrection, and for the conclusions they would draw from it, by a pre-Christian Jewish set of concepts in which figures of various sorts might be seen to play a quasi-divine role, though such figures do indeed flit through our literature and at least one of them—the figure of "Lady Wisdom"—is almost certainly one of the influences on both Paul and John in the way they talk about Jesus. But "Wisdom" in ancient Jewish thought, both biblical and post-biblical, is a way of talking about *the wise purposes of Israel's God and the intention of Israel's God to come back in a new way to dwell with his people.*

That points us in the same direction as the one I just mentioned. I do not think that the direction of travel, so to speak, was that the first Christians were thinking about Jesus and found themselves driven to speak of him as somehow within the divine identity. I think they were thinking of the long-awaited personal action of Israel's God in history to overcome the powers of evil. When they were confronted, to their incredulous astonishment, with the resurrection of Jesus, they were forced very quickly, by a rich combination of searching the scriptures on the one hand and worship and prayer on the other, to conclude that Israel's God had indeed acted within their history, shockingly, surprisingly, unexpectedly, compelling a fresh reading and reappraisal of everything they thought they knew.

At the heart of all this was the belief that in order to tell the story of what this one God had done, and how he had done it, they had to tell the story of Jesus. They had to speak (and perhaps to sing; some of the earliest relevant material is a sort of poetry) of the choices he made, the life he lived, and particularly the death he died. The resurrection of Jesus thus burst upon the hermeneutical world of first-century Jews, not least the well-stocked mind of a Pharisee like Saul of Tarsus, shedding new and unexpected light on passages of scripture they knew but may never have read like that before. The resurrection compelled them to tell the story of God and God's people in a whole new way. That, I think, was the origin of early, high, Jewish Christology. It was a story about Israel's God doing at last what he had promised; and it was a story whose central character was Jesus of Nazareth.

A good example of the way in which all this happened can be seen in the early Christian use of 2 Samuel 7, in which the prophet Nathan brings to David the divine answer to the proposal that he, David, should build a house for Israel's God. On the contrary, says Nathan,

> The Lord declares to you that the Lord will make you a house. When your days are fulfilled and you lie down with your ancestors, I will raise up your offspring after you, who shall come forth from your body, and I will establish his kingdom. He shall build a house for my name, and I will establish the throne of his kingdom for ever. I will be a father to him, and he shall be a son to me.
>
> (2 Samuel 7:11-14)

This passage, together with Psalm 2 and similar texts, is known to have been used in the context of messianic expectation, for instance at Qumran. But the early Christians, including we may assume Paul himself, saw in it a meaning that, so far as we know, no previous reader had thought of. In the clause "I will raise up your offspring after you," the word "I will raise up" is *wehaqimothi* in Hebrew. This in itself carries no particular overtones, any more than when, in common American usage, someone says "I was *raised* in New York," such a

speaker is not envisaging any vertical movement. But when the
early Christians read the Septuagint, the Greek they read was
kai anastēsō to sperma sou. By itself this could be heard, like the
Hebrew, without any dramatic change of meaning. God would
"raise up" a new generation, a new heir for David, presumably
referring to Solomon, the one who would build the house (as
in v. 13). But the early Christians, startled into fresh readings
of familiar texts by the unprecedented and unanticipated event
of Jesus' resurrection, would have found this text full of new
meaning: I will *resurrect* your seed. This is almost certainly the
explanation for the coupling of Davidic promises with resurrection, with the whole idea of the new Temple, and with the
belief that Jesus was "son of God." But the phrase "son of God"
was heard not only in the Davidic sense, as in this passage and
obvious texts like Psalm 2:7 and Psalm 89:27, but also in a
dramatically new sense, itself unprecedented but, as with the
idea of a crucified Messiah, unveiled in the resurrection. *Jesus
had done what Israel's God said he would do in person.* The resurrection, demonstrating victory over death itself and hence
the launching of new creation, compelled the first Christians
to bring together several elements which by themselves would
not have precipitated this result. Jesus' own way of calling God
"father," coupled with previously unnoticed scriptural clues on
the one hand and the experience of his presence in worship on
the other, led very quickly not so much to the belief that Jesus
was the *messenger* of Israel's God, a kind of plenipotentiary
emissary, but to the belief that he was actually the *embodiment*
of Israel's God, doing at last what he had all along said he
would do, though in a completely unanticipated way.

All this is behind the scenes, as it were, in the dense opening formula of Paul's letter to the Romans:

> . . . the good news about his son, who was descended from
> David's seed in terms of flesh, and who was marked out

powerfully as God's son in terms of the spirit of holiness by
the resurrection of the dead: Jesus, the Messiah, our Lord!

(Romans 1:3-4)

In the days when scholars were eager to split off Paul's own
thought from that of putative early "Jewish Christians," it was
fashionable to suggest that the reference to David in this passage was simply a throwback, echoing a time in early Christianity when Jesus' Davidic Messiahship had been important,
but now "corrected" by Paul with a different idea, that of a
divine "sonship." I do indeed think it likely that Paul is here
echoing a very early formula. But he is doing so, not to correct it, but to use it as the foundation for everything that is
to come in the letter. The formula as it now stands encapsu-
lates exactly the train of thought I have just been describing,
holding together the Davidic Messiahship which remains vital
and central to Paul's picture of Jesus (as it continued to do, we
note, throughout the Christianity of the first century at least)
with the quite new belief, backed by the new implicit exegesis,
which had been called into play by the resurrection itself. The
event which Paul and the other early Christians saw as the
divine declaration "this really was my son," validating the messianic claims which had otherwise been trampled underfoot in
the crucifixion, was also the event which compelled the fresh
reading of scripture. The formula as it stands thus looks on
exactly to the restatement at the start of chapter 9, where Paul
describes Jesus in a similarly double way:

It is from them, according to the flesh, that the Messiah
has come—who is God over all, blessed forever. Amen!

(Romans 9:5)

The meaning of both passages, 1:3-4 and 9:5, is held in
place by the sense of the argument that follows. In Romans
1–8, as could be shown in detail, Paul holds together the sense

that in Jesus as Messiah Israel's vocation and destiny are real-
ised and the sense that in this same Jesus the rescuing love of
Israel's God has appeared in person to suffer in his flesh the
condemnation of "sin":

> The law of the spirit of life in the Messiah, Jesus, released
> you from the law of sin and death. For God has done what
> the law (being weak because of human flesh) was incapable
> of doing. God sent his own son in the likeness of sinful
> flesh, and as a sin-offering, and, right there in the flesh, he
> condemned sin.
>
> (Romans 8:2-3)

Similar things could be said about Galatians 4:4 and other
relevant passages. That is for another time. My argument here
is simple. It was not the case that there was a well-known body
of scriptural texts which, before the time of Jesus, were understood to be predicting the coming of a "son of God" who would
be raised from the dead. It is the case (a) that there were several well-known texts which were seen as predicting a coming
Davidic Messiah; (b) that some of these well-known texts seem
to have been ignored altogether by the early Christians (we
hear next to nothing in the New Testament, perhaps surprisingly, of the "sceptre" promise of Genesis 49:10 or the "star"
promise of Numbers 24:17); (c) that some of these well-known
texts, with 2 Samuel 7 as my chosen example, were seen in a
new and startling light as a result of Jesus' actual resurrection.

All this is instructive, not just about Christology itself, but
as an example of wider issues. We cannot construct a tem-
plate of Second-Temple Jewish faith and life and see it as a
smooth progression in which Jesus simply appears, does what
everyone knew the scriptures said he ought to do, and is hailed
by his followers as having fulfilled their scripturally based
expectations. The cross says "No!" to any such suggestion, just
as loudly as Karl Barth said it to Emil Brunner. But nor can

we suggest that the resurrection created ex nihilo the belief that Jesus was Israel's Messiah and the embodiment of Israel's God. *The resurrection meant what it meant within the context of Second-Temple Jewish worship, hopes, expectations, and readings of scripture. But it transformed each of those in unexpected and indeed disturbing ways.*

In particular, the resurrection of Jesus, and this fresh retrieval of latent meanings of "son of God," points to a theme which has I think been insufficiently explored. Here again there is a delicate balance between "what people would have said in the Second-Temple period" and "what the early Christians quickly came to say about Jesus." We cannot in any case generalise and say that *all* Second-Temple Jews embraced this or that belief. But there are strong hints in both the exilic and post-exilic scriptures, and then in the wider Second-Temple post-biblical literature, that many saw the promises of the glorious return of Israel's God as being yet unfulfilled. Ezekiel promised that the divine glory would return to the rebuilt Temple, but nobody in the Second-Temple period ever said it had happened. Isaiah 40:5, 9-11 speaks of Israel's God coming back at last, with his glory visible to all the world, ruling the nations with judgment and gentleness. That promise is repeated as the long poem we call Isaiah 40–55 nears its climax:

> Listen! Your sentinels lift up their voices,
> together they sing for joy;
> for in plain sight they see
> the return of YHWH to Zion.

(Isaiah 52:8)

Again, however, there are no texts indicating any claim that this event has happened. The glorious visible presence of Israel's God had not returned. That is why, after the rebuilding of the Temple, prophets like Zechariah and Malachi continue to affirm that he *will* come back—and to warn against carelessness in the apparently ambiguous present time (Zechariah 2:10-11; Malachi 3:1-2). The only text known to us that claims that some kind of divine "return" has happened is Sirach 24, where the figure of "Wisdom" is sent to dwell in the Temple.

Does this mean that nobody in the Second-Temple period believed that Israel's God was present within that Second Temple? Not in so many words. Just as today those who gather for prayer at the western wall of the old Temple in Jerusalem will sometimes speak of a sense of divine presence, even in the grief of nearly two millennia of desolation, so we may assume that those who sang the Psalms, who offered sacrifices, who brought gifts to the Temple in the time of Jesus and Paul, would have had a similar sense. Jesus himself, as reported by Matthew 23:21, speaks of the Temple as the place where God lives (though several manuscripts read "used to live"). But it is noticeable that nobody ever says that the great prophecies just mentioned have been fulfilled. And it is particularly noticeable that later, when one of the Rabbis is giving a list of the ways in which the Second Temple was inferior to the First Temple, the one built by Solomon, the *Shekinah* is mentioned as among the things which had been in the First Temple but were not in the second. The "glorious presence," the shining "tabernacling," was not there. One might hazard a guess that this was an ex post facto deduction: had the *Shekinah* been there, how could the Romans have destroyed the Temple? That could have been dealt with by an explanation like that in Ezekiel 10: the divine glory abandoned the sanctuary because of the wickedness of the people. Something like that may lie behind the strange stories in Josephus about the great gates opening and celestial voices being heard declaring that they were leaving. At the very least I think we have to say that there was a puzzle at the heart of Israel's worship, a puzzle to do with apparently unfulfilled prophecies of the glorious return of Israel's God to the sanctuary; and that, whatever a straw poll of worshipers at the Temple would have concluded on the matter, the early

Christians were quite clear that these prophecies—Isaiah 40, Malachi 3, and the like—had been startlingly fulfilled in the coming of Jesus. The evidence is found right across the New Testament. Once more, this evidence does not point to a fixed and well-known body of texts which had simply to be invoked for everyone to get the message. It points to the high probability that the resurrection of Jesus, demonstrating that the victory over death had been won by the man some had believed to be Messiah, compelled the followers of Jesus to the conclusion that this victory over death itself must be the work of Israel's God in person, and to join together in fresh exegetical patterns texts that had spoken of the glorious return.

We can see this in Mark 1:2-3, picked up by the other Synoptics. John makes the same point in his own way, speaking of the Word that becomes flesh and "tabernacles" in our midst, so that "we gazed upon his glory" (John 1:14). Paul comes at the same notion in a wide variety of ways, using in particular the language of the Exodus, the time when Israel's God went with his people in the pillar of cloud and fire to lead them to their "inheritance." Indeed, as we have seen, the theme of "new Exodus" is never far away from the mind of Paul, or indeed of other early Christians. Like many other themes, the Christology we find in many passages seems to grow out of early Christian reflection on what it means to say that the new Exodus did in fact take place when Jesus came out of the tomb on the third day after his crucifixion. All this is true as well, by the way, of what Paul says about the Spirit, but there is no space here to explore that.

All this is to suggest once more that we should see the rise of early Christology, with Paul as its earliest definite witness, neither as a fresh creation out of nothing, nor as a simple extension of ideas already widely believed in theory and merely requiring concrete exemplification. The resurrection created a new situation in which Jesus' followers were pushed into new reflections, new searchings of scripture, new patterns of prayer. But the reflections, the scriptures, and the prayers were themselves rooted in the earlier Jewish traditions, even though the new configurations were unanticipated. A major new piece had been added to the jigsaw, and now at last—so the early Christians believed—the existing pieces, which many had struggled to put together in this way or that, could at last fit together to form a picture which both was and wasn't the one they had been expecting.

Of course, all this compelled Paul and the others to push at the borders of language. They must have known they were doing that, but they had no choice. Paul speaks of the one God, but he speaks of this God as the one who sent the Son, and the one who sent the Spirit of the Son—and then declares to the Galatians that they have now "come to know God—or, better, to *be* known by God" (Galatians 4:9).

This extraordinary exploration, a quest for fresh meaning right at the heart of ancient Jewish belief, was not undertaken out of a desire for the development of speculative theory. Study of the early Pauline communities has shown that one of the things that held together the very disparate groups of Jesus-believers was precisely their monotheism, striking both in its firm opposition to the normal polytheism of the pagan environment and in its extraordinary inclusion of Jesus, and of the Spirit, within the meaning of the "one God." In other words, the revised monotheism of Paul and his communities had a *social* rather than a merely *speculative* function. Part of this is what is meant by a belief being formed in worship, since the worship itself was, for Paul, supposed to be an expression of the unity of the church across traditional social barriers. Part of it has to do with the definition of the community: after all, once the barriers were down, what marked out this unexpected collocation of unlikely people? For Paul, as we indicated earlier, the answer was this belief: confessing that Jesus was *kyrios*, and believing in "the God who raised Jesus from the dead."

3

APOCALYPTIC

Covenantal Narrative or Cosmic Invasion?

Recent American study of Paul, picking up from some earlier Continental discussions, has raised very sharply the question: was Paul an "apocalyptic" thinker? Was he, perhaps, an "apocalyptist"? Did he belong to a movement called "apocalypticism"? Is this the hidden clue that unlocks those parts of his thought which might otherwise remain hidden, leaving us only with a shallow and overpersonalised "gospel" about the individual rather than about the massive and sometimes monstrous issues of the wider world?

This proposal has been sharply polarised into two either/or questions, which we must investigate in the present chapter:

a. Is Paul invoking an "apocalyptic" worldview which rules out a "covenantal" narrative?

—or, more particularly,

Does Paul see the cross and resurrection of Jesus as the divine "invasion" which brings to an end the narrative of Israel's covenant with God, and begins

a new non-covenantal era in which the dark powers which have ruled the world are defeated?

b. or, Is "apocalyptic" simply a literary form which does not necessarily determine the worldview being expressed?

—again more particularly,

Can the cross and resurrection of Jesus invoke Israel's covenantal narrative in a way which shows at the same time how the "cosmic" powers are dealt with?

Let us first see at least some of the evidence for saying that we must factor in to any account of Paul a larger context which might be called "apocalyptic"—first noting what that might mean. The word "apocalyptic" comes from the Greek *apokalypsis*, which is a general term meaning "revelation," the unveiling of something previously hidden. It is found at the start of the "book of Revelation," the final book in the New Testament canon, and from there it has been used to describe other similar books, particularly Daniel and parts of Ezekiel in Israel's scriptures and works like *1 Enoch* and *4 Ezra* in the Second-Temple writings. From there it has broadened out to include the hypothetical worldview of an entire swathe of Second-Temple Jewish thought. This scholarly development occurred particularly in the late nineteenth century, when most people working on the relevant texts thought such a worldview a dark, dangerous development, declining away from the sunlit uplands of the earlier "prophetic" theology. But with the dark, dangerous days of the twentieth century there came a dramatic reversal: suddenly texts that had formerly been pushed to one side were retrieved. They matched the mood of the times. Suddenly people wanted to hear about "apocalyptic."

And some wanted Paul to be an "apocalypticist." They had had enough of a shrunken quest for personal "authenticity." That had not prevented the multiple horrors of the twentieth century. Perhaps Paul would provide a fresh sense that even when human affairs seemed to be the plaything of dark forces beyond our control, even these forces had been defeated on the cross.

The evidence was not hard to find, in some of the best-loved parts of Paul's writing. It was not just that he spoke of the *parousia* of Jesus, of him descending from heaven with a cry and the archangel's trump (1 Thessalonians 4:16). It was not simply that he spoke (or at least that someone writing in his name spoke) of a "man of lawlessness" being revealed, making himself out to be a god (2 Thessalonians 2:3-4). The former is common early Christian tradition; the latter could be pushed aside as secondary. It is not even that Paul writes of being "citizens of heaven," waiting eagerly for the saviour to come from there (Philippians 3:20). It is, rather, that we find again and again in Paul two things which are also found in many of the Jewish writings to which the label "apocalyptic" has often been applied: the "two ages," on the one hand, and the "three agents," on the other.

Take the "two ages" first. We quoted in an earlier chapter from Galatians 1 and 6. In 1:4 Paul speaks of the effect of Jesus' death being "to rescue us from the present evil age"; in 6:15, "what matters is new creation." The famous "But now" of Romans 3:21 indicates that Paul marks a sharp distinction between the former time and the new time of the gospel. The equally famous line in 2 Corinthians 5:16-17 speaks of the great divide: once upon a time, we looked at things in the old way, but now there is a new kind of "knowing," because there is a new creation. And so on.

So too with the "three agents." Some philosophical schemes—and, alas, some theological schemes—see the drama of life as a two-agent story, with "God" and "humanity" playing out a zero-sum game. Everything is done either by the one or the other. Humans are given responsibility, a choice, free will to use this way or that, and they will be held accountable for their "sin" if they misuse this freedom; and then, in some schemes, they are rescued from this sin and its consequences by a mechanism of atonement. Not so, according to the "apocalyptic" Paul. There are three agents in this drama, the third one being the collective appearance of dark forces. There is Sin with a capital "S," not simply "sins" as the sum total of the freely chosen human misdeeds; there is Death with a capital "D," not simply the collective chaos of all human demise. There are other powers, too, dark forces standing behind, or above, the human drama and making their presence felt. They matter enough for Paul to celebrate their incapacity following the death of Jesus:

> I am persuaded, you see, that neither death nor life, nor angels nor rulers, nor the present, nor the future, nor powers, nor height, nor depth, nor any other creature will be able to separate us from the love of God in King Jesus our Lord.

> (Romans 8:38-39)

Some of these "powers" have enslaved people in the past and will threaten to do so again, even after the people of God have been rescued through the gospel events:

> When we were children, we were kept in "slavery" under the "elements of the world." But when the fullness of time arrived, God sent out his son. . . .
> But now that you've come to know God . . . how can you turn back again to that weak and poverty-stricken lineup of elements that you want to serve all over again?

> (Galatians 4:3-4, 9)

As the letter to the Ephesians puts it:

The warfare we're engaged in . . . isn't against flesh and blood. It's against the leaders, against the authorities, against the powers that rule the world in this dark age, against the wicked spiritual elements in the heavenly places.

(Ephesians 6:12)

Sometimes this cosmic opposition takes human form:

The satan himself transforms himself to look like an angel of light, so it isn't surprising if his servants transform themselves to look like servants of righteousness.

(2 Corinthians 11:14-15)

And the whole picture is moving toward a final showdown in which the victory won on the cross and demonstrated in the resurrection will be worked out once and for all:

The Messiah rises as the first fruits; then those who belong to the Messiah will rise at the time of his royal arrival [parousia]. Then comes the end, the goal, when he hands over the kingly rule to God the father, when he has destroyed all rule and all authority and power. He has to go on ruling, you see, until "he has put all his enemies under his feet." Death is the last enemy to be destroyed, because "he has put all things in order under his feet." But when it says that everything is put in order under him, it's obvious that this doesn't include the one who put every-thing in order under him. No: when everything is put in order under him, then the son himself will be placed in proper order under the one who placed everything in order under him, so that God may be all in all.

(1 Corinthians 15:23-28)

All this and much, much more indicates that Paul did indeed believe (a) that the full story could not be told without factoring in the "powers" which are bent on corruption and death and the victory over those powers which God achieved through Jesus, and (b) that the events of cross and resurrection constituted the decisive moment in world history, when God acted in a fresh way to break the grip of the "powers" and to rescue people from them, ushering in the "new age" or the "age to come."

There is even more. When Paul is talking about the effect of his gospel, he speaks of the "apocalypse," the "unveiling," of God's "righteousness" and also his "wrath":

> The good news . . . is God's power, bringing salvation. . . . This is because God's *dikaiosynē* is unveiled [*apokalyptetai*] in it, from faithfulness to faithfulness. . . . For the *orgē* of God is unveiled [*apokalyptetai*] from heaven against all the ungodliness and injustice.

> (Romans 1:16-18)

(I have left *dikaiosynē* and *orgē* untranslated; the traditional renderings are "righteousness" on the one hand and "wrath" on the other.) And, though the word used is different, Paul says much the same thing in his famous "But now" in Romans 3:21: "But now, quite apart from the law (though the law and the prophets bore witness to it), God's *dikaiosynē* has been displayed [*pephanerōtai*]." Paul seems to envisage that both with the decisive events of the cross and the resurrection, and then with the equally decisive moment when these events are announced by the evangelist, there occurs a cosmic disclosure in which, behind the sad and messy story of a young Jewish preacher being executed by the occupying forces, the audience suddenly sees "what was really going on." This was the unveiling of the divine "righteousness." Of course, it would be good to know at the same time what Paul meant by this most controversial of his technical terms, but many scholars have suggested that "righteousness," too, is an "apocalyptic" term concerned with the divine power going to work in the world to overthrow the forces of darkness and to create a new world of "salvation."

Paul uses similar language to speak of the extraordinary moment in his own life in which he was transformed from persecutor to preacher. His gospel came "through an unveiling [*apokalypsis*] of Jesus the Messiah," because God "was pleased to unveil [*apokalypsai*] his son in me" (Galatians 1:12, 15). Paul uses the same word-group on several other occasions.

If we are to give this evidence full weight, and if we are to suppose Paul to have been even moderately consistent as a thinker (this has, of course, been challenged, but with any writer we must start by supposing that they at least think they are making sense), then there are some things we must assume that Paul did not believe. He did not believe, for instance, in the kind of view we mentioned before, in which human life is seen as a straightforward "deal" between God and humans: God makes the rules, humans either keep them or not, God either punishes them or forgives them. Things appear much more complicated than that, to put it mildly.

But, equally importantly, the features we have sketched rule out the possibility that Paul might have seen human history, and particularly the history of Israel, in the way that some nineteenth-century thinkers wanted to see it, as a kind of immanent process through which "history" as a whole, or perhaps something called "salvation history," would work its way forwards with an inexorable power, achieving a smooth crescendo toward a climax. The toxic combination of Hegel and Darwin, as developed by many thinkers, both Christian and non-Christian, produced various beliefs like this, fueling the worldviews through which people came to believe that having a European war in 1914 was a good idea, then fueling the idea that either the Russian revolution of 1917 or the rise of the Nazi party in the 1930s was the inevitable outworking of historical forces, leading to some kind of secular paradise. (If it seems now incredible that anyone should have thought like that, it merely shows how quickly and radically worldviews can change.) Clearly, if Paul had known about any such views, including any would-be "Christian" versions of such views, his "apocalyptic" theology, as sketched in briefest outline about, would rule them out.

Third, if these elements are genuine, they form central parts of the way Paul understood how it was that God's purposes for the world were not confined to one particular small group. The word "cosmic" is of course fuzzy. It can refer to the entire created universe as investigated by modern science, or it can refer to the entire world of suprahuman powers that may be there even though modern science cannot investigate them, or it can simply refer to the whole of our planet and all creatures who live here. But whichever route we go in terms of that word, Paul's vision of God's action in the death and resurrection of Jesus, and the full effects of that action, cannot be contained in the small world of one segment of the human race, or in a system of "salvation" which depends on some people figuring out what they need to "believe" in order, somehow, to escape the consequences of their sins. Thus, what began as a protest of one school of German theology against another—a postwar protest, in the light of the "revelation" of wickedness that had become all too apparent, against what seemed the smaller human-centred ideas that had been current before the war—has turned into a major American movement in which the small concerns of this or that group as to what constitutes "right belief" or the proper "way of salvation" are outflanked by a Pauline, "cosmic" vision. In this vision, all the powers of Sin and Death have been defeated by the divine "invasion" of the world in Jesus and his death and resurrection.

Much of this picture is compelling. But there are problems with it as a complete account of what Paul is all about. Let me first sketch a hypothetical equal-and-opposite point of view.

For a start, there is something odd about appealing to Paul's use of the Greek word *apokalypsis* and its cognates as though we could infer from this ancient word that Paul embraced something we now call "apocalyptic" or even "apocalypticism." Paul never mentions such a "movement" or worldview. Nor does anyone else in the period. Josephus lists the parties and groups in the Jewish world of his day, but "apocalypticism" is not among them. It is a modern construct. Paul can easily use the same language for a variety of other purposes; as, for instance, when he says that he went up to Jerusalem "because of a revelation [apokalypsis]" in Galatians 2:2, or that God would "reveal" to the Philippian Christians things they still needed to know (Philippians 3:15). When the Psalms, which Paul knew very well, prayed that God would "open my eyes" (apokalypson tous ophthalmous mou, Psalm 119 [LXX 118]:18), nobody then or now would take this as a signal that the Psalmist was embracing the kind of worldview some might call "apocalypticism."

For another thing, the Jewish idea of "two ages," and the equally Jewish idea of "three agents" (or at least a sense that "God" and "humans" are not the only agents in the drama of life), are found across a wide spectrum of Jewish literature, by no means only in works which we might call "apocalyptic." Both themes are prominent in the later writings of the Rabbis, from whose thought "apocalyptic" notions were regularly excluded, since they were seen as part of the dangerous—and dangerously political!—way of writing which some people reckoned had contributed to the twin disasters of AD 70 and 135. If one wanted to find classic statements of "the present age" and "the age to come," one could indeed go to 4 Ezra. One could equally well go to the anti-"apocalyptic" Rabbis.

The mention of the political understandings of "apocalyptic" writings leads to a further point that is strangely absent from the new American "apocalyptic" school. Books like Daniel, 1 Enoch, and 4 Ezra were not concerned with "salvation" in any normal western sense ("how to go to heaven when you die"), nor yet with the mechanisms of how such a

thing might be accomplished. They are much more directly
about the social and political crises facing the Jews in the last
centuries before, and the first century after, the time of Jesus.
They use the lurid imagery of "apocalyptic" to *denote* the
actual political realities, world empires, haughty tyrants, and
so on, and to *connote* the fact that behind these human agents
there stood dark powers bent on destruction, especially for
the little embattled people of God. The "political" reference
does not cancel out the reference to suprahuman powers.
It contextualises these writings in ways which the current
American debate about Paul has not done. It demonstrates
that one cannot simply go to "apocalyptic" texts as though
they are addressing, far less answering, the normal modern
questions of western, and particularly Protestant, soteriology.
The works I just mentioned are not trying to ask, Do people
"get saved" because of a cataclysmic divine action, or do they
have to be "justified by faith"? They are asking, How, in the
present crisis, will the one God keep his promises and bring
his justice and mercy to Israel and the world?

The modern questions about how "salvation" happens
loom large in the current debate. Sometimes we have seen
a putative "apocalyptic" played off against something called
"justification theory," as though there are two distinct theological paths between which a vital and exclusive choice has to
be made. Sometimes it appears that what is meant by "apocalyptic" is simply a sweeping reference to the divine sovereignty
over all human affairs, and in the event of salvation particularly, at which point one might wonder how this differs from
the great Reformational emphases of Luther and Calvin, and
whether what we are seeing is simply a new way of addressing
the traditional questions of grace, faith, and "works." This is
especially troubling when, in some supposedly "apocalyptic"
readings of Galatians in particular, we find ourselves back in
the world of post-Reformation polemic, in which the "teachers" whom Paul is opposing are insisting on a "religion" rather

than a "revelation," the implication being that the "works"-
based Jewish world of these "teachers" is the problem to which
Paul's fresh "revelation" is the answer. This always runs the
risk of falling back into the so-called "old perspective," and
thus needing once more the critique of Stendahl, Sanders, and
others.

There is a particular irony here. When we study the Jewish world from which Paul came, we find plenty of "apocalyptic" but hardly any mention of "justification." That is one
of the reasons why an earlier generation rejected the former
and embraced the latter: for that school of thought, the less
Jewish the better! Now, however, the situation is reversed, and
"apocalyptic" is held up as the alternative way—the superior
way!—of understanding Paul, so that "justification" is either
subtly transformed into "rectification" or is pushed aside altogether. There are many confusions here.

All this might well lead us to the conclusion that "apocalyptic" was never a worldview or a movement at all, but only
a literary genre. And the point about a literary genre is that,
though it could sometimes suggest what the subject matter
might be, it would not dictate it. If someone were to write a
line or two in metres such as Shakespeare used to do, that
wouldn't tell us what we'd want to know about the characters,
the plot, the show: Was this a drama? Did it break your heart
with heroine and hero soon to part? Or was it just a sonnet,
made in jest, to tease the ear with fancies and the rest? Or did
it just stop short, leaving you wondering what went wrong?
John Bunyan wrote *Pilgrim's Progress* as if it was a dream he
had had; but it wasn't. It was a method, a literary device. Plenty
of other writers have used the device of "I had a dream" without launching into an allegory of Christian salvation. Is there
any solid evidence to demonstrate that all the "apocalypses"
we have, whether Christian or Jewish or anything else, shared
a common *worldview* which was not also shared by many
other movements in the Jewish world of the day? Was there

ever, in short, anything—any group of friends, any movement continuing through a few generations, any teaching or
sustained scriptural exposition—which would deserve to be
called "apocalypticism," and to be marked off in that way from
all the other expressions of Jewish life and thought which we
can trace in this period? It is arguments such as these, coupled
with the manifest confusions evident in some of the loose uses
of the word "apocalyptic" by scholars over the last century,
which have caused some to opt for the minimalist solution,
and to say that the word really ought to be confined to the
literary form alone, the form we find in Daniel 7–12 or in the
sequence of visions in 4 Ezra.

We know how this form works, and, granted the caveat
above, what at least some of its likely content might be. The
seer has a dream or vision. An angel stands by to interpret, to
explain the puzzling and disturbing nightmare that the seer
has had—much like Joseph interpreting Pharaoh's dream in
Genesis 41, or like Daniel himself interpreting Nebuchadnez-
zar's dreams in chapters 2 and 4 and then reading the writing
on Belshazzar's wall in chapter 5. (In Daniel, unlike most other
such books, the seer who interprets dreams and visions in chapters 1–6 becomes the dreamer whose visions require angelic
interpretation in chapters 7–12.) The interpretations—both
Daniel's interpretations of the royal dreams and the angelic
interpretations of Daniel's dreams—concern not simply the
"heavenly world" of a normally unseen supramundane reality
but the combination of the real mundane world of monarchs
and empires *together with* the equally real, but supramundane,
world of principalities and powers. It is *both* "political" and
"cosmic." Again and again in such visions, Israel's God demonstrates his sovereignty over the nations and their rulers by setting up a kingdom which cannot be shaken.

Nowhere does Paul write anything in this literary form.
He neither offers interpretations of someone else's visions nor
reports a dream or vision which an angel or someone else has

interpreted to him. To be sure, some of the sorts of things revealed in Daniel or *4 Ezra* are prominent in his writings. First Corinthians 15, quoted above, looks in that direction; so does Romans 8. So, for that matter, do several passages in 1 and 2 Thessalonians—though we note that there, as in Romans 2 and several other passages, Paul, like the tradition of Jewish "apocalypses," is clear about a coming day of judgment in which "the wicked" will be condemned, a point strangely absent in the implicit universalism of the modern American "apocalyptic." The whole tradition of Jewish "apocalyptic" writing regularly highlights both "politics" and "the judgment of the wicked." Arguably, Paul does too. But the modern attempted retrieval keeps them both at arm's length.

At one point, to be sure, Paul mentions visions and revelations, and indicates that he (or just possibly someone else) has had wonderful "mystical" experiences. But their content remains secret. The passage in question, 2 Corinthians 12:1-5, is actually an *anti*-apocalypse: the expected public disclosure never takes place. If there was a "revelation," it remained secret. It would be somewhat bizarre to give the name "apocalyptic"— that is, "revelation"—to a passage which explicitly refuses to reveal to the reader what was heard in the heavenly realms which the seer had supposedly visited.

The mention of actual mystical experience, however, points to a more subtle set of distinctions through which, perhaps, we may start to find a creative third way between the rather sharp antithesis posed at the start of this chapter. We know from later sources that several Jews in several periods engaged in various practices of meditation, whether concentrating on the throne-chariot described in Ezekiel 1, or on the name of God, or on other heavenly mysteries or gateways to such mysteries. We can safely assume that the rich traditions of prayer visible in later Jewish writings go back, in some form or another, to Paul's day. Devout Jews like him really did hope for, and seek to obtain, the kind of vision or revelation hinted at in 2 Corinthians 12. But neither this practice, nor any writing about it, give us reason to infer the presence of a movement such as what today is called "apocalypticism." As with the "two ages" or the "three agents" sometimes cited as the vital signs of "apocalyptic," the practice of "mysticism" is not confined to any one group. Nor is it associated with the clearly demarcated worldview produced out of the blessed rage for categorisation on the part of some nineteenth-century scholars.

It may well be—as with much ancient history, this is lost to our sight—that part of the origin of "apocalyptic" literature is to be found in such mystical experiences. It is difficult to tell, without some external clues, whether an account of a dream or vision is a report of an actual personal experience or whether, like Bunyan's "dream," this is simply a convenient and perhaps evocative literary form. One way or another, it appears that there are at least four things going on. First, some people have real dreams or visions, and they write about them. Second, some other people have something they want to say, which they want to invest with a supposedly "inspired" quality, and they use the form of the vision-literature to achieve this end, perhaps placing the vision, or its interpretation, in the mouth of a hero from an earlier age (Enoch, Ezra, Daniel). Third, many if not most of the second category, and perhaps the first as well, are searching for the supramundane clues which will explain, and help people navigate, disturbing or chaotic events both national and global. Fourth, writings of this type are regularly used to declare that, despite appearances, the God of Israel, the creator of the whole world, is actually in charge, and though at the moment things are dark and terrifying, there will come a time of great reversal, of judgment and rescue.

Three conclusions follow directly from all of this. First, the belief just mentioned—the hope of fresh divine action to smash through the chaos and bring about new creation—was widely held, in one form or another, by many different Jewish groups in Paul's day. Perhaps only the Sadducees, anxious for their social and political standing, would have resisted it. Even the post-135 Rabbis, horrified at the disaster that had come about through the more overtly political versions of this belief, continued to think in terms of "the present age" and "the age to come"; of course they did, since they still believed that Israel's God was the creator of the world and was therefore responsible for its ultimate putting-right. Hope like this could be expressed in a variety of literary forms, or indeed nonliterary symbols such as the Temple and its liturgies and festivals and/or loyalty to Torah. It did not mark off one particular group ("apocalypticism") from other groups and movements known to us in this period.

Second, it is abundantly clear that Paul himself believed in this idea of fresh divine action doing something dramatic through which the whole world would become—had already become!—a different place. For Paul, however, this event had split into two: the death and resurrection of Jesus was the decisive moment, but the ultimate overthrow of corruption and death itself, at Jesus' *parousia*, would in its way be equally decisive. Paul believed that "the present time" was a different *kind* of time, an overlap of the ages.

Third, however, for Paul as for those of his Jewish contemporaries who believed in this kind of sudden, cataclysmic divine action, this was never set over against the belief in the fulfilment of ancient promises. When the great moment burst upon the unready world, it would nevertheless fulfil the divine promises made in ancient times to Israel's forebears.

Here we touch upon the great oversimplification forced upon us (I believe) by the philosophical and political muddles and disasters of the last two centuries. *Both* the Hegelian schemes of F. C. Baur, in which "history" was an immanent process of dialectic between opposing forces, moving eventually to a synthesis, *and* the countertradition of "salvation history" maintained by some through (perhaps) to the work of Oscar Cullmann, thought in terms of an inexorable "progress," an inner movement, perhaps of a "progressive revelation," in which all one would really have to do would be to wait for the music to build up to its great climax. There is no sense of that in Paul.

For Paul, the messianic events of Jesus' death and resurrection, and indeed the ultimate future dénouement at the *parousia*, were much more like the crashing chord a few bars from the start of the slow movement of Haydn's "Surprise Symphony." Haydn's trick—first lulling a postprandial audience into gentle slumber, then waking them up with a fright— does however illustrate the more subtle thing that is going on. The *sudden volume* of the chord interrupts the previous diminuendo. It brutally "invades" it, shattering previous implicit expectations. But the chord itself belongs quite properly with the preceding *harmonic sequence*. It sums it up and prepares for what is to come. The movement with its simple tune is in C major; the chord at the end of a natural progression is the dominant, G major. It is not as though Haydn suddenly wrote a chord of D flat minor or something completely dissonant, as though the late twentieth century were suddenly to intrude upon the late eighteenth.

This, of course, is only an illustration. It may not catch all of what is going on in Paul. But the sense that something has happened which dramatically disrupts the sequence while also, in another dimension, bringing it to its promised completion—that is true to Paul. *How* we say that, so as not to collapse into a nineteenth-century immanent progress on the one hand or a twentieth-century cataclysm on the other, is the hermeneutical challenge of "apocalyptic" in our day. *That* we must say something like this ought not to be in doubt.

This means, in particular, that we must avoid at all costs the false antithesis between "apocalyptic" and *the promises and purposes of the covenant God of Israel*. Which "God," after all, are we talking about? To say that "God has invaded the world," or something similar, is to raise this question sharply. Is this just any "God"? For Paul, of course, it is Israel's God, the creator of the world. But as soon as we say that we are faced with the problem: if the one who invades is the creator, Israel's God, has he changed his mind? Was the covenant with Israel a radical false step? The fact that Paul rather obviously wrestles with these questions, in Romans and Galatians in particular, indicates that he is attempting to hold together things which many interpreters (in many different traditions!) have allowed to fall apart.

Here we touch on a theme which we will develop in the next chapter, but for the moment we must at least say this. In all the Jewish "apocalypses" known to us, the longing for the great new moment, the divine "invasion" through which the world will be held to account and radically transformed, is generated by the belief that *Israel's God is indeed the world's creator, and what this God will do for the world will somehow relate to what he will do for Israel, and vice versa.* Daniel and his friends long for the "return from exile," for the overthrow of the wicked powers that rule the world; the Jewish hope nests within the cosmic vision—and, in some sense or other, actually drives it. In the great vision of Daniel 7, the exaltation of "one like a son of man" (whether interpreted messianically or in terms of Israel as a people or indeed some kind of "true Israel") is the means by which the "monsters" will be destroyed. The "apocalyptic" writings do not give us the one without the other. Yes, it is always possible for "covenant" hopes to become inward-looking, to generate a private world which could then, under certain circumstances (modern western individualism, for instance) become a fussy little place where one's own "salvation" was the only thing that mattered. (This seems to be a particular *bête noir* of some of the American "apocalyptic" school: one must make Paul an "apocalyptist" in order to avoid individualistic fundamentalism.)

One might perhaps see that danger in some of the Qumran scrolls, though they often express, as well, a sense of the

coming reordering of the whole world. With Paul the balance
is always maintained. The "apocalyptic" argument of the letter
to the Galatians hinges vitally on Paul's fresh interpretation of
the Abraham story, particularly Genesis 12 and 15. There, as
Paul reads the story, God makes promises to Abraham concerning all the nations, and the specific promises concerning
"family" and "land" are interpreted in that light, anticipat-
ing the larger and fuller argument of Romans, in which the
covenant fulfilment of chapters 3 and 4 leads directly to, and
should not be played off against, the cosmic vision of chapters 5–8. This obviously depends on a much longer exegetical
argument about both letters and a much fuller linguistic and
thematic analysis of the elements within them, but it seems to
me vital for a robust historical reading of Paul's writings and
his main themes.

The trick is, I think, to make it clear that for Paul the "covenant" language, focused on but by no means confined to the
discussions of Abraham in Romans and Galatians (we should
certainly include 2 Corinthians 3 here as well), is never, for
him, about a charmed circle of friends enjoying a "salvation"
away from the rest of the world. It is always about the ancient
divine plan to rescue the whole world from its corruption and
decay, to put right the problem facing the whole human race
and hence to put right the problem which has engulfed the
whole world. After all, whoever put together the book of Genesis in its final form, they and their intelligent readers knew,
from the sheer narrative flow, that what was being said in Genesis 12 and onwards constituted the divine answer to the problem of Genesis 3–11.

What then is this global problem, and how does Paul
envisage it? This is the last element of the present discussion
about "apocalyptic." At this point the debate has become
bundled up with a larger contemporary theological discussion, owing much to Barth: does Christian theology think
"forwards" or "backwards"? Does it start with the world and

an analysis of its problems and possibilities, working "forwards" to the "solution" (or perhaps the "climax") in Jesus?
Or does it start with Jesus and work "backwards" to a fresh
understanding of "what was always the case" and/or "what
was always the problem"? If it begins with the problematic
nature of the present world, how can it avoid importing dis-
torted categories into its "solution"?

The American "apocalyptic" school has insisted, rightly
in my view, that Paul worked "backwards." For him, the
death and resurrection of Jesus had shed a flood of new and
unexpected light on everything, including the meaning of
creation and the nature of its plight. This, after all, is what
Paul meant when he said that the gospel reveals not only the
"righteousness" of God but also, and in semantic parallel, the
"wrath" of God (Romans 1:17, 18). Paul does not start with
a "neutral" view of the world and its problems and work up
to Jesus, however much various interpretative traditions have
tried to teach and preach Romans 1–4 in that way. That was
one of the reasons for starting the present book with a consideration of Paul's view of Jesus. It embodies in the present
literary form (echoing other earlier and longer attempts) the
principle I am expounding.

But this does not mean, and did not mean for Paul, either
that those who had never heard of Jesus had no sense of a
"plight" or a "problem," or that any such sense they might have
had is quite different from what Paul now articulates. When
we look both at the literature of the wider world (Epictetus,
Seneca, other contemporaries of Paul, and the writings to
which they were indebted) and also at the writings of the Jewish world, we are aware of all kinds of expressions of "plight."
Death is the ultimate one, of course. The Epicurean attempts
to deny the fact actually subtly reinforce it. But non-Jewish and
Jewish thought alike points the finger at other things, too: the
corruptions of power, the arrogance and accidents of empire,
the strange moral lapses even of otherwise virtuous persons.

People in all cultures have always been aware of these things and much more.

In Jewish literature everything looks back ultimately to the opening chapters of Genesis, where the sad and dark events of Genesis 3–11 are held between the opening vision of the human project (as a key part of the whole creation-project) and the surprising new turn in the call of Abraham in chapter 12. Thus the stories of the forbidden fruit in Genesis 3, of Cain's murder of Abel in chapter 4, of the invasion of the "sons of God" in chapter 6 and the consequent spread of wickedness in human hearts and lives, and then not least of the Tower of Babel in chapter 11—all this remains a single, complex, interlocking repository of ancient Israelite reflection on "the problem," the "plight" from which humans in general, Israel in particular, and beyond both the earth itself are in need of rescue.

Does Paul echo all this? Obviously yes. Adam, death, wickedness, dark "powers," empire—they are all there (though some who emphasise the "powers" have tried to use that as an argument against including "empire"). Is he, to that extent, echoing Jewish "apocalyptic" writings in which similar retrievals are made? Yes, of course—though he, like they, can only say one thing at a time, and must leave the integration of the complex themes to the reader. Has he revised his thinking on all these things—Adam, death, the "powers," empire—in the light of what he believes about Jesus, his death and resurrection, his inauguration of the kingdom of God? Yes, of course. The crashing chord interrupts the sequence of *volume*, though not the sequence of *harmony*. The problem of Genesis 3, 4, 6, and 11 remains; but now Paul has been woken from his previous slumber to see it all with new eyes—and to offer and explain the new solution, which could never have been guessed at by even the most devout Pharisee but which, he believes, has now been unveiled, revealed, disclosed in the gospel.

It is therefore misleading to play off Paul's language about human "sin" (individual misdeeds and the sum total of such misdeeds) and his language about "Sin" as a power, a dark force impinging on human life from the outside. Such a disjunction has commonly been made in pietistic individualism, highlighting the former and playing down the latter, sustaining a soteriology in which God deals with "sins" by punishing Jesus for them. The disjunction is no less acute, and no less unwarranted, when, in order to avoid that kind of distortion, one highlights the latter and plays down the former, suggesting that what really matters is Sin as a power which has now been defeated in the death of Jesus, sustaining a "Christus Victor" soteriology. (That does rather give the game away. One of the best-known theological debates of the mid-twentieth century was between Gustaf Aulén in his "Christus Victor" proposal and the previously widespread view of some kind of Anselmic "satisfaction" theory. The new "apocalyptic" proposals are, to this extent, an attempt to substantiate an Aulén-like repudiation of Anselm in terms of Pauline exegesis. Aulén's work, however, is problematic and oversimplified. The present attempts to replicate it exegetically share these deficiencies.) Paul works with both models—indeed, to see them as two different "models" is itself, I think, to collapse his more supple thought and expression, couched as it often is in narrative, into the flat, one-dimensional either/or of abstract theory.

This is not the time to explain how all this works out. But we can at least see one passage, by common consent a major summary of Paul's message, in which both elements, and many others too, for that matter, are held together:

> So, therefore, there is no condemnation for those in the Messiah, Jesus! Why not? Because the law of the spirit of life in the Messiah, Jesus, released you from the law of sin and death.

> For God has done what the law (being weak because of human flesh) was incapable of doing. God sent his own son in the likeness of sinful flesh, and as a sin-offering; and, right there in the flesh, he condemned sin. This was in order that the right and proper verdict of the law could be fulfilled in us, as we live not according to the flesh but according to the spirit.
>
> (Romans 8:1-4)

There is much in this dense summary which goes beyond our present purposes. But we can see here, clearly stated and closely integrated, the two things which current debates have split apart. First, God condemned "sin" in the flesh of Jesus the Messiah, so that "there is no condemnation for those in the Messiah." That language is both "penal" and "substitutionary," though we should note, against some crude expressions, that Paul does not say "God condemned Jesus," but that he "condemned sin" in the flesh of Jesus. But the context is all to do with "Sin"—sin as a dark power that must be "condemned," not simply the accumulation of individual misdeeds.

This follows of course from Romans 7, in which "sin" is both a power that uses the Law to capture, enslave, and kill humans, and also the result of that enslavement in terms of actual human misdeeds. *The effect of Sin's power is that humans commit "sins" and so are enslaved, corrupted, and killed.* With hindsight from what he has learned through the gospel, Paul sees more clearly the problem of which he, like most first-century Jews, was already aware. That is why, in both Romans 6 and Romans 8, Paul's supposedly "apocalyptic" message about what has happened through the Messiah's death and resurrection results in the repeated and robust instruction: because you are no longer under the power of Sin, you must no longer commit sin. Both are important, and in Paul we can see how the two work together.

In particular, Paul sees that "the problem" was *deeper* and *more radical* than he had before imagined. Reconstructing what Paul might have thought in his "former life as a Pharisee" is fraught with problems, but there are many texts, including Qumran, the Psalms of Solomon, and so on, where we might well get the impression that "the problem" is simply that the non-Jewish world worships idols and so behaves in a less-than-fully human fashion, and that some Jews are joining the non-Jewish world in its wickedness. The Rabbis sometimes speak like this as well. This then funds the *political* critique and question: why are the wicked idolaters running the world, and what will the creator, Israel's God, do about it?

One can easily imagine first-century Jews reading a book like Daniel and seeing there this kind of critique—and a "solution" which would involve a fresh divine action to confront the wicked pagans (and their renegade Jewish collaborators), break their power, and rescue God's people from their grip. What we see in Paul, and for that matter in 4 *Ezra*, is something deeper and darker. The crucifixion and resurrection of Israel's Messiah teaches Paul something new. *Israel itself is "in Adam"*; that is, the problem which might have been thought to be purely external, a problem against which Torah, properly observed, would have protected God's people, turns out to be deeper, and to have infected not just the pagans but the whole human race, Israel included. For 4 *Ezra*, it looks as though the destruction of Jerusalem by the Romans has had a similar effect. The problem is worse than we had imagined; it must go all the way back to Adam himself. That is the move being made, not a transition from a "cosmic" soteriology to a "forensic" one. When the recent "apocalyptic" school cites 4 *Ezra*, as it sometimes does, as a representative of a particular kind of "forensic apocalyptic" in which the mention of Adam triggers a train of thought to do with a "two-agent" scheme (humans sin; God punishes them or perhaps forgives them), what we miss is a sense of the historical context. Just as the messianic events concerning Jesus caused Paul radically to deepen his implicit critique of the world to include the same critique of Israel itself, so the destruction of Jerusalem precipitated a similar crisis in some Jewish thinkers of the late first and early second centuries.

In Pauline terms, therefore, we cannot say that "apocalyptic" must be played off against "covenant theology." That suggestion belongs with certain ill-formed debates of the mid-twentieth century, not with the historical study of the first century. We cannot say that the "vertical invasion" of the gospel events rules out any sense of ongoing history. For Paul, the death and resurrection of Jesus are the radically new event, the new centre of everything; but the point is that they happened "when the fullness of time arrived" (Galatians 4:4). Only by holding all this together can we understand just how radical his apocalyptic gospel really was.

We have now referred quite often to Paul's view of Israel, the covenant, and the law. Once it is clear that such reference is not rendered redundant by the appeal to "apocalyptic," the way is clear to a fresh understanding of Paul's vision of the people of God, and of the key doctrine of "justification," which explains who those people are and how they come to that status.

4

THE JUSTIFIED PEOPLE OF GOD

Messianic Israel or Saved Sinners?

Everything we have said so far indicates that we must now focus attention on the question of the people of God in Paul's thought. Here there are two different questions which have dominated discussion, often conducted as though the other did not exist but needing to be held together if either is to be properly addressed.

Even to summarise these questions is to risk distortion, but the attempt must be made:

> **a. Does Paul see the people of God as a company of "saved sinners," a new group who, being "justified by faith" rather than "by works of the law," have left behind everything to do with "Israel according to the flesh"?**

Or does that get the whole picture wrong? Might it not rather be something like this:

> **b. Or does Paul see the people of God as in some sense the "new Israel," envisaging a kind of**

transformation through which the people of God
as a whole, not merely individuals, have been
turned through Jesus' death and resurrection into
something new?

Before we even take the first steps to explaining this dilemma
and addressing it, we note one disturbing fact. *Both of these
positions can be expressed in terms which end up being, or at least
being seen as, anti-Jewish.* Granted the climate of our times, in
which the long memories of the Holocaust rightly dominate
our horizon, that is something we all want to avoid. But the
issues are not simple. Some distinctions must be made.

Some of those who take the first option stand in a long
line, going back to Martin Luther and behind him to the
mediaeval period, in which "the Jews" are seen as "the problem" and the church is seen as the answer. The notorious stat-
ues of the blindfolded synagogue and the clear-seeing church,
outside the cathedral in Strasbourg and elsewhere, sum this
up. Christianity is a different sort of religion; a superior sort.
It has taken the place of Judaism in the purposes of God. This
generates the horrid old sneer, "How odd of God to choose the
Jews." The whimsical addition of "and not the Scot" does not,
to put it mildly, mitigate the problem. This position generates,
and then sustains, readings of Paul in which, for instance,
the soteriology of Romans chapters 1–4 or even 1–8 is highlighted and the agony of chapters 9–11 is quietly set aside as
a problem for Paul but not for us. It should be obvious that
this view, long soaked into both Christian and post-Christian
western culture, both Catholic and Protestant (and also into
some Eastern Orthodox culture, though that is outside my
province), has been responsible for some of the greatest evil
the world has ever seen.

Some of those who take the first option above, however,
end up with a different view. Some in the "dispensation-
alist" movements continue on the one hand to live by the

individualist and fundamentalist gospel of saved souls who have had a faith-experience leading them to abandon their "works" and be assured of "going to heaven," while on the other hand combining this with a contemporary political stance in which the present state of Israel can do no wrong. I regard this as a severe distortion both theologically and politically. This view, however, seldom makes its way very far into serious scholarship.

The American "apocalyptic" school is compromised at this point. Martyn's commentary on Galatians makes it clear: his Paul rejects the message of the infiltrating "Teachers," because they are offering a "religious" package while he is offering something quite different. This can be nuanced in various ways, but as we have seen it always threatens to collapse back into some version of the so-called "old perspective," in which Judaism is the wrong sort of religion and Paul is articulating— well, if not the right sort, because this "Paul" does not teach "religion"—nevertheless "something better." Something superior. Something which, just as much as the older view, leaves "Judaism" behind.

Even Ed Sanders' famous book *Paul and Palestinian Judaism* runs the risk of perpetuating a mild version of the same phenomenon. "This is what Paul finds wrong with Judaism," he writes in a famous conclusion: "that it is not Christianity." Paul did not, according to Sanders, find anything actually "wrong" with "Judaism"; the appearance of any "critique" is simply a retrospective reaction, the invention of a "plight" in the light of the "solution." Sanders, it is true, explains much of Paul's thought within, rather than over against, Jewish categories, though actually his book is a comparison of patterns of religion, not an attempt to describe the genealogy of ideas. He does not invoke the categories of Hellenistic religion to explain why Paul says what he does. But he still regards Pauline Christianity and "Judaism" as two quite different sorts of thing. Pauline Christianity, for him, is a "third race," neither really Jewish nor really Greek.

The first view, in whatever variation, thus lives with the problem that the saving plan of God appears to involve leaving "Judaism" behind and embracing something else. It was this way of seeing things, developed massively in the work and the legacy of F. C. Baur, that caused generations of writers to look for antecedents to Paul's thought, not in the Jewish world, but in the non-Jewish "religious" sphere of either the mystery religions or the imperial cult or Gnosticism. Pauline "Christianity" was to be non-Jewish by definition. That was part of a worldview now fairly thoroughly discredited, and however sophisticated the attempted retrieval, it will always carry those problems.

The second view, however, is frequently attacked on similar grounds. To suggest that Paul envisages the church as a "new Israel," or perhaps a "true" or even "renewed" Israel, going in any way beyond the confines of mainstream first-century Judaism (always supposing we can be sure what that was), is regularly deemed to be just as bad as the first view. Granted, such a view emphasises that Paul saw himself as still very much a Jew; that he was consciously retrieving Jewish traditions and locating his ecclesiology within the Jewish world, rather than outside it as in the first view; that in his mature work (particularly Romans) he presents a nuanced vision of the Jewish law rather than appearing to reject it. Some have plausibly argued that we should see the event on the road to Damascus not as a "conversion" in which he swapped one "religion" for another, but as a "call" in which the God he had always worshiped was now summoning him to a new set of tasks. All this would mean that, over against the first view, Paul would be understood in a sense "within," rather than "over against," the Jewish world of his day.

Such readings, which come in various shapes and sizes, look back to two great works of earlier days: Albert Schweitzer's

The Mysticism of Paul the Apostle and W. D. Davies' *Paul and Rabbinic Judaism.* In the latter, particularly, Paul fits so well within the Jewish world of a reconstructed proto-rabbinic movement (that reconstruction seems much more difficult to us today than it did to Davies) that he seems to have no real critique of his former life at all. Davies gives little or no attention to the passages, such as Romans 2:17-29 or Philippians 3:2-11, not to mention Galatians as a whole, in which Paul appears to be putting clear water between himself and the way of life he had left behind. This is one kind of challenge that this second view faces.

In meeting these challenges, however, this second view splits into at least two options. In the first, for which Krister Stendahl is a back marker, Paul was offering gentiles a way of access to Israel's God without implying that Jews who did not recognise Jesus as Messiah were somehow at a disadvantage. Jews could stay Jews and gentiles could become Christians. The attractions of this view in the world of western relativism in general and post-Holocaust anxiety in particular are obvious. Its weaknesses *as a proposed historical reconstruction of Paul* are also obvious. There is Galatians for a start. There is the question of why, if that was Paul's view, he had "great sorrow and endless pain in my heart" because of the unbelief of his flesh-and-blood relatives (Romans 9:2-3) and prayed fervently that they might be saved (10:1, at the start of a section which makes it clear that this "salvation" will come through faith in Jesus as Messiah). One can of course say, and many have done so, that when Paul says "all Israel shall be saved" in Romans 11:26 he is explaining that, after all, his earlier agony was unnecessary, and his earlier prayers too anxious, because there will come a time when all without exception will be saved. That solves one problem at the cost of creating several others.

Anyway, the difficulties of sustaining a view like that of Krister Stendahl have led others, the present writer included, to conclude that for Paul at least the effect of the gospel on the ancient people of God was that it was *transformed and expanded*. When non-Jews came to faith in Jesus, they did not become something else other than (in some sense) "Israel." Paul speaks clearly in Romans 9:6 of an "Israel" and another "Israel," and in the chapters that follows he arguably explains this distinction in detail. Paul also speaks of "our ancestors," referring to Moses and his contemporaries, in addressing a largely gentile audience in 1 Corinthians 10:1: he is there, so to speak, narrating gentile converts into the larger story of "Israel," and it is noticeable that having just done that, he refers to the continuing Jewish world as "Israel according to the flesh" (1 Corinthians 10:18). If Paul's communities were in some sense a "third race," as seems to be indicated at the end of the same passage ("Be blameless before Jews and Greeks and the church of God," 1 Corinthians 10:32), this community nevertheless was to go on telling its self-identifying story as the story of Abraham, Isaac, Jacob, Moses . . . and the Messiah. How very Jewish; and yet, because of the Messiah, how very much transformed.

This "transformation" or "enlargement," however, has itself been seen as another classic type of "supersessionism," the apparent "replacement" of the Jewish people by something else, namely "the church." However hard one tries to indicate and emphasise that Paul affirmed the Jewish beliefs in the creator God, the covenant with Abraham and Israel, the goodness of the Torah, and the basic Jewishness of his communities; however much one stresses the Jewishness of the ethics Paul inculcates (rejection of idolatry and sexual immorality still being central) and the hope he teaches (resurrection); some will still cherish a lingering suspicion that there remains here a latent form of anti-Judaism. Some, in the attempt to ward off such a charge, are prepared to allow that Paul himself still followed the kosher food laws and expected other Jewish Christians to do the same, though this becomes harder to discuss because there is often disagreement as to how those laws were applied, in the Jewish Diaspora, when Jews and non-Jews were to eat together (or, as according to Galatians 2:11-14 happened in Antioch, when Cephas and others decided that it was wrong to do so).

In order to get any further with these difficult and contentious questions, it will be helpful to bring in the other related discussion, which, for many, is still *the* discussion about Paul: what did he mean by "justification by faith"? There is a sense in which the so-called "new perspective" on Paul is one particular sharp edge of the second position I have outlined, though, as I just suggested, Ed Sanders, the godfather if not the grandfather of the "new perspective," is still in some sense part of the first position. But this particular pair of questions, as a subset of the first pair, can be put like this:

c. When Paul speaks of "justification," is he talking of the "imputation of Christ's righteousness" to the believer despite the absence of meritorious "works"?

Or, as in at least some varieties of "new perspective,"

d. When Paul speaks of "justification," is he speaking of the inclusion of all believers, gentiles as well as Jews, within the single family who are to share table-fellowship?

As I say, I have come to share Albert Schweitzer's view of the placing of these questions. For him, "justification" was a smaller "crater" located within the larger "crater" of "being in Christ." Forensic theology was a subset of incorporative or participatory theology. There are many ways of saying this, but they come back, in swirling clouds of argument, exegesis, and putative history-of-religions parallels, to the same sort of thing. Are these categories—the law court on the one hand, the incorporation into Christ on the other—mutually exclusive? Are they different metaphor systems which sit alongside one another somewhat uncomfortably, both referring to some third system in which things might be held together a bit more easily? Or what?

To all of these questions, the pair with which I opened the present chapter and the pair I have just set out, Paul would offer a single basic starting-point from which to work up to answers. *Jesus of Nazareth was and is Israel's Messiah.* His resurrection revealed it, validating in a shocking reversal the implicit claim throughout Jesus' public career, and the sneering announcement nailed to the cross. To the first position, which has always tended to forget Paul's Jewish context, and for whom therefore the word *Christos* simply became a proper name, perhaps being transformed en route into a quasi-divine title, Paul would say No: what Jesus has accomplished he has accomplished as Israel's Messiah. Paul's shorthand summary of the gospel in 1 Corinthians 15 does not begin "Jesus died for our sins." It begins "The Messiah died for our sins." Hardly surprising, since twice in the short formula he says that this happened "in accordance with the scriptures." Somehow, in ways that the first position never really begins to recognise, the "salvation" accomplished by Jesus is related in Paul's mind to the fact that Jesus brought to a head the long purposes of Israel's God.

It is not enough to gesture, as the first position sometimes does, to Israel's scriptures as possessing some earlier random examples of "justification by faith." Here Sanders' attempt to expound Romans 4, suggesting that Paul simply ransacked his scripture-soaked memory for texts that linked "righteousness" and "faith," without regard for their contexts, is more or less at the same level as the exegesis of the Protestants he normally opposes. Nor will it do to say that though Paul does allude to, or echo, earlier "Jewish Christian" doctrinal formulae, he of course modifies them away from their original and still unfortunately "Jewish" meaning. If Paul quotes, he quotes because the quotation says exactly what he wants to say; and, after all, Paul is himself a "Jewish Christian," and to suggest otherwise is to collapse back once more into the position of F. C. Baur. That is the trouble, actually, with older western readings of Paul, both Protestant and Catholic, both liberal and conservative. They have screened out the basic Jewishness of Paul's message, of which seeing Jesus as Messiah is a key symptom, and have thus cut off the branch on which they should have been sitting.

The same point—Paul's belief in Jesus' Messiahship—is the central thing to be said in relation to the second approach outlined above. Did Paul think that Jesus was Israel's Messiah? To be sure. Even those, like Martin Hengel, who continued to say that Messiahship plays no significant role in Paul's theology have agreed that Paul did indeed believe that Jesus was Israel's Messiah; and the combination of the "messianic" texts alluded to by Paul, the "messianic" *arguments* advanced by Paul, and the wider messianic overtones in all parts of early Christianity right across the first century—all this indicates that Paul certainly did regard Jesus as Messiah and, what is more, made this belief loadbearing in his theological understanding, in ways I will shortly explore. But we then have to ask: if a first-century Jew, particularly a scripturally literate one, came to believe that this or that person was the divinely appointed Messiah of Israel, how would this play out in terms of everything else they believed? Would they ever be able to say, "Yes, this person (Judah, Simeon, Baruch, whoever) is the Messiah, but don't worry too much; those of us who believe he is the Messiah will follow him, but the rest of you can do your own thing?" Of course not. One of the reasons that, as Josephus says with sorrow, more Jews were killed in the war of 66–70 by other Jews than by the Romans themselves was that to claim that Israel's God was acting in *this* way, here and now, through *this* person, meant that rival claims were ruled out: ruled out in theory, to be ruled out in practice by violence where necessary. When Akiba hailed Simeon ben-Kosiba as Messiah in 132, this could never be a matter of saying, "Some of us think Simeon is Messiah, others of you will disagree, so let us agree to differ." If Simeon is Messiah, he is already king of Israel, and demands allegiance. That is clear enough in the letters he wrote, and, even more poignantly, in the coins he had struck, with the years "1," then "2," then "3." That is what a messianic claim does. It restarts the calendar.

To that extent, if one is going to grasp the nettle, one must say that all Jewish renewal movements of the period were in their very essence "supersessionist." They all claimed that Israel's God was acting *here* and *now* and *in this way* and *with these symbols* rather than somewhere else, by some other means, and with some other signs. Those who decided to stick with "somewhere else" would be left behind. That was true of Qumran. It was true of the Pharisees (though the debates between Hillel and Shammai may, even if we could reconstruct them accurately, reflect what both sides saw as allowable differences). It was certainly true when the Mishnah, after declaring that "[a]ll Israel has a share in the age to come," provided a list of exceptions, including of course the Sadducees (*Sanhedrin* 10:1). A Messiah could never be just another teacher from whom Israel might learn certain truths, might gain fresh wisdom. This is why, in a famous quip of the Jewish scholar Jon Levenson, the most Jewish thing about early Christianity was precisely its "supersessionism." If the Messiah has come, it means that Israel is in some sense being regrouped, reformed, *transformed* around him.

Transformed: yes, indeed. The second key point is that for Paul Israel's Messiah is the Jesus who had not only been raised from the dead but who had been crucified. Now one might still argue that even if Jesus really was raised from the dead, and even if that did indeed constitute him as Israel's Messiah, one need not pay much attention to the manner of his death.

One need not draw drastic theological or ecclesial conclusions from it. That might be a possible position in theory, but one could never argue that it was Paul's. For Paul, the crucifixion of the Messiah carried immediate implications for the very identity of Israel on the one hand and, on the other, for the non-Jews who came to faith in him. That is why, as he says,

> The word of the cross, you see, is madness to people who are being destroyed. But to us—those who are being saved—it is God's power . . . Jews look for signs, you see, and Greeks search for wisdom; but we announce the crucified Messiah, a scandal to Jews and folly to gentiles, but to those who are called, Jews and Greeks alike, the Messiah—God's power and God's wisdom.
>
> (1 Corinthians 1:18, 22-24)

The "scandal" of the cross meant trouble for Paul. It resulted in physical persecution, hostility, misunderstanding, death threats. This was not just because the message offended people's sensibilities. In the harsh Roman world of the first century, people were used to all sorts of brutality. The word of the cross was a "scandal to Jews" because it said loud and clear, as only a powerful symbol can, that the way into God's new creation, for Jew as well as gentile, came through dying and coming alive again. The Messiah had lived out—as only with hindsight one could recognise—what the divine purpose had been all along. When Paul says that the Messiah's cross means that the world has been crucified to him, and he to the world (Galatians 6:14), he is applying specifically what he said about himself, but also by implication about all Jews who came to believe in Jesus as Messiah and to be baptised:

> Through the law I died to the law, so that I might live to God. I have been crucified with the Messiah. I am, how-ever, alive—but it isn't me any longer; it's the Messiah who lives in me. And the life I do still live in the flesh, I live

within the faithfulness of the son of God, who loved me
and gave himself for me.

(Galatians 2:19-20)

To pretend otherwise—to suppose that for Paul the crucifixion of the Messiah was simply an atoning mechanism without
larger sociological implication, or whatever—is not only to fail
to read the text. It is to invite Paul's own rebuke, that one is
trying to avoid persecution for the Messiah's cross.

To focus in this way on Paul's belief that Jesus was Israel's
Messiah, and that his crucifixion was not simply an unfortu-
nate prelude to his revelation in that royal role but rather was
itself a revelation—an "apocalypse," one might say!—of the
divine saving plan, the divine "righteousness," is therefore to
find the way in to Paul's vision of the renewed people of God.
Scholars for the last generation and more have tiptoed around
phrases like "new Israel" or "true Israel" or "renewed Israel,"
because they have been naturally and properly anxious about
any lapse back into a world of thought (usually a non-messianic
world of thought) in which "the church replaces Israel." Once
we put the Messiah in the middle of the picture, however, it
is clear that this is not in Paul's mind. *The Messiah sums up
Israel in himself.* The Messiah is Israel-in-person. Did Paul
believe that Jesus was Israel's Messiah? Of course he did. Did
that mean that Israel was redefined around this Messiah? Of
course it did. Does that mean that Paul or those who repeat
this line of thought are anti-Jewish? Of course not.

There is, however, a problem with the claim that the Messiah represents Israel. It appears to be unsupported by contemporary evidence. Nowhere that I know, whether in Qumran or
the Psalms of Solomon, whether in Josephus' descriptions of
would-be "Messiahs" in the first century or in such evidence
as we have about bar-Kochba—nowhere do we find anything
explicit about a fluidity between the Messiah and the people of God. Older attempts to invoke a kind of "corporate

personality" have been attacked on the grounds of adopting outdated anthropological assumptions. Biblical evidence I have cited before, not least the language about people being "in David" or "in the son of Jesse" (2 Samuel 20:1; 1 Kings 12:16, the latter all the more interesting because it comes two generations after David's death), is all very well, but we do not see these passages being retrieved in Paul's day to form part of a standard "messianic" expectation.

Here again, as in earlier chapters, we face the problem of innovation from within, cognate with the other regular problem of critique from within. I would still be prepared to argue from Paul's remarkable "incorporative" language, and in particular from the way in which he uses *Christos* as the focus of this "incorporation," that the hypothesis of a fluidity between Messiah and Israel explains the data better than anything else I know. But I would now rest still more weight on a point I made in an earlier chapter. *Paul as a Pharisee expected that God would raise all Israel from the dead at the end of time; but God had raised Jesus from the dead in the middle of time; Paul therefore concluded that what God had been going to do for Israel, he had done for Jesus. Jesus, thereby declared to be Messiah, was therefore Israel-in-person.* Once again the resurrection is the epistemological starting-point. I do not think Paul grew up with a ready-made incorporative idea of the Messiah, though he may well have noticed how, in the stories of David, the young king-in-waiting went by himself to fight Goliath on behalf of Israel. Paul certainly started with a well-defined notion of "the hope of Israel" in terms of "resurrection"; but the actual resurrection of Jesus shed a new light on that. I think, therefore, that the resurrection of Jesus pointed Paul *both* to Jesus' Messiahship *and* to the incorporative nature of that Messiahship. That explains at a stroke all the detailed argumentation about his language of "in the Messiah," "with the Messiah," and so on.

But if—after that detour—we accept both that Paul believed Jesus to be Israel's Messiah and that his resurrection indicated that he was Israel in person, then there can be no question of suggesting that Paul, or his interpreters, are "replacing" Israel with something else. Israel is not replaced, but *represented*, by the Messiah. And *then all those who belong to the Messiah are themselves part of the single people of God.* That is how Romans 2:25-29 works. That is how Galatians 3 and 4 make sense. That is why Paul's language about the church in 1 Corinthians 10 means what it means.

All this suggests that, though exegetes and theologians will go on facing the temptation to treat as "replacement" what for Paul is "representation," it must be firmly resisted. Going on emphasising the Messiahship of Jesus is a start. Resisting the strange notion that Jesus is the "Christian Messiah" as opposed to the "Jewish Messiah" (no such distinction was ever imagined, certainly not by Paul) is necessary. Cashing out the claim that Jesus was the one Messiah of Israel in terms of an actual people, an actual inheritance, over against the "spiritualising" tendencies of so much western Christianity, is vital. (Those tendencies are, to be sure, why many Jews have said that this seems to them to be a different kind of Messiahship.) For Paul, the church is what it is, and means what it means, because it is "in the Messiah," who has summed up Israel in himself: Israel's identity, Israel's vocation, Israel's destiny. This remains scandalous, but we must be sure to locate the scandal at the right point. For Paul, it is focused on the cross.

All this means—and this is central and vital for the whole debate, though routinely ignored—that when we are talking about "Paul and Judaism," *we are not talking about "religion," but about eschatology.* We are not lining up—Paul was not lining up!—one "religion" and comparing it with another. This is where, ironically, the great modernist project of "comparative religion" drives us not into tolerance but into intolerance. We may start by imagining that we are placing two things side by side and observing their differences. But it can never stop there, at least not for anyone with any kind of affiliation to one "side" or the other. It will end with "comparison": this or that aspect of the one is superior, or inferior, to the equivalent aspect of the other.

That is not how Paul's mind worked; not in his treatment of the Jewish law, not at all. For him, what mattered was, as we have seen all along, that something had *happened* as a result of which the world was a different place, the scriptures had to be read differently, new creation had begun, and even knowledge itself had been transformed. To this extent, Paul was in the same position as Akiba after hailing bar-Kochba as Messiah. The kingdom had begun. It was time—*time!*—to restart the calendar. We have been misled once more by the nineteenth-century proposal that Christianity and Judaism were two types of this newly invented thing called a "religion," which bears only a passing resemblance to anything the word "religion" might have meant in the first century. Within a renewal movement, a "messianic" movement, any "critique" of those who refuse to join in is not because they have the wrong system, the wrong "religion," but because they are living in the wrong time zone. They are still asleep in bed when the sun has already risen.

But of course the new time is not straightforwardly discontinuous with everything that had gone before. All the renewal movements for which we have evidence, whether Qumran or the Pharisees or the waves of rebellion in the first century, and on to the last fateful revolution, were all concerned with the appropriate retrieval of Israel's scriptures. If this was the moment of fulfilment, there would be, for sure, a fresh sense that the prophecies had come true, that Torah was being kept in a new way, that Israel was somehow being reconstituted. This is exactly what we find in Paul. And this brings us to another contentious point.

I have tried to emphasise that Paul did not arrive on the road to Damascus with his head full of a single, solid and coherent scheme, needing only the name of Jesus to be added for the picture to result in his mature theology. Far from it. I have insisted that the resurrection of the crucified Jesus caused him to rethink from the ground up everything he had ever believed, from his own sense of who he was right up to his increasingly dramatic sense of who God was. I have stressed that though we can track many things in Second-Temple Jewish readings of scripture that might have influenced him, there are some prominent themes in his Jewish world which do not reappear in his writings and some prominent themes in his writings which do not obviously seem to have a parallel in his Jewish world. But there is one feature of his mature thought which, though like everything else it has been rethought in the light of the resurrection of the crucified Jesus, is far more prominent in the Second-Temple world than is normally believed, and which I have tried with mixed success to bring to bear on the relevant discussions. This is the "long exile," the idea that, in line with Daniel 9, many if not most Jews of Paul's day believed that they were still waiting for the fulfilment of the great prophecies which, in Isaiah, Jeremiah, and Ezekiel, spoke of the glorious return of Israel not just to the land but to a state of freedom, and also of the glorious return of Israel's God to the Temple.

This point is well known among scholars of Second-Temple Judaism. I first met it in the 1980s, in Michael Knibb's commentary on the Qumran Scrolls and in Michael Stone's seminar in Jerusalem. It seemed obvious to them, though not to many New Testament scholars for whom "Judaism" was still a kind of "background" rather than a narrative which might be going somewhere, that most Second-Temple Jews saw themselves living in the elongated moment of "exile" spoken of in Daniel 9. It was only gradually, and particularly through starting to see how some Jewish writers of the time linked that chapter with the covenant sequence of curse and blessing in Deuteronomy 27–30, that I came to see its potential for understanding Paul. There is still, I think, enormous resistance—not only among those who embrace the newer "apocalypticism," though obviously there especially—to any idea of continuity between the new world envisaged by Paul and the ancient Jewish world. For many readers, the suggestion that there might be a *single continuous story* is ruled out either on Protestant principles (we know that God breaks in and does something new) or on "apocalyptic" principles (a continuous story would mean an immanent development).

The point, however, is that for Paul (a) there is indeed a continuous story, from Abraham to the Messiah and on into the messianic future, but that (b) there is a dark interval in which the promises made to the patriarchs, and the promises set out in the prophets, seem to have passed through a deep valley, a time of sorrow and judgment and exile and death. *The continuous exile guarantees that the new creation cannot simply be the climax of the old world.* It must be about reversal, about sudden renewal, about the startling fulfilment of ancient promises through and despite Israel being in the worst place imaginable. There is a narrative which runs from Abraham to the Messiah, but it must pass through the valley of the shadow of death. As Paul says in Romans 11:6, if it were not so, "grace would not be grace." Apocalypse would not be apocalyptic. Apocalyptic gospel and continuing exile need one another for the full Pauline sense to be discerned.

This brings us by a circuitous route to a different and still more fundamental point about the Jewish narrative. Again, to be sure, different Jews told the story of Israel in different ways. We can see this going on in the New Testament. Matthew 1 whisks us through the story from Abraham, to David, to the exile, and to the Messiah (an interesting sequence, by the way) with the simple though subtle device of a genealogy. Stephen, in Acts 7, tells the story from Abraham to the Messiah while highlighting in particular the Israelites' original rejection of Moses and the biblical warnings against absolutising the Temple (since "the Most High does not live in shrines made by human hands" [v. 48]). Chapter 11 of the letter to the Hebrews takes the story back as far as Abel, taking in Abraham and plenty of others en route but still arriving at the Messiah. This spread of evidence, before we even look at Paul, indicates that various ways of telling the story of Israel were current among the early Christians; was this a new thing? Did the Christians invent this kind of narrative despite the fact that Jewish communities had not done any such thing?

Of course not. The Bible itself contains not only the large narrative from Genesis to 2 Kings, with Ezra and Nehemiah as a supplement and the books of the Maccabees offering different kinds of later updating. It also contains many smaller passages in which different ways of telling the story were tried for different purposes. Psalms 105 and 106 are typical, the former telling the story of the Exodus as a splendid triumph, the latter going back over the same narrative from (as it were) the seamy side, with Israel constantly getting it wrong. Once we get into the postbiblical world, there are many more such retellings. They are all different, for different purposes, but most of them do three things: they (1) recall the ancient promises in order (2) to reaffirm their validity for the present day and (3) to stir up Jews to loyalty and courage to face the immediate challenge.

These stories come in many forms, from apocalyptic visions like Daniel 7 or the long retellings in *1 Enoch* or *2 Baruch* through to the actual history writing of Josephus. Since we meet fresh, Jesus-focused retellings of the same story elsewhere in the New Testament, on what grounds would we deny that Paul might have done the same sort of thing? If the answer is, "because Paul gave up everything Jewish to gain Christ" (echoing Philippians 3:7-11), we must reply that at that very moment, and at various other points in the letter, he is still telling the Jewish story—or rather, the radically new version of it which has been precipitated by the messianic events concerning Jesus.

This is the point, once again. Here, quite differently from the matter of incorporative Messiahship, there is an abundance of Second-Temple evidence for Jews telling their long story, replete with dark intervals and tragic episodes and always an abiding sense of hopes dashed and raised and dashed again. The closest we get to a Second-Temple telling of the Jewish story in which things build steadily toward a glorious climax is in ben-Sirach, and it is hard to suppose that this book, so obviously glorifying the temple hierarchy, was popular by the time of Paul or in the circles he frequented as a young man. Even so, although there is a long tradition of Jewish storytelling, once again we must insist that Paul starts from the resurrection of the crucified Messiah. This does not, of course, mean that he can ignore everything that has gone before. Once again, the Messiah's death and resurrection mean what they mean "in accordance with the scriptures," even though he now reads those scriptures in accordance with the Messiah. So he tells the story . . . from Adam, to Abraham, to Moses, to the exile, to the Messiah.

He does this in different ways for different purposes. Galatians 3:6–4:7 is clear: this is the story of Abraham, through Moses, to the Messiah, wrestling on the way with the question of the relationship between Abraham and Moses (God promised Abraham a single family, but Moses, through Torah, would have created two different families—corresponding of course to the two different families that would result from a table-separation in Antioch or Galatia). Moses and his Torah were the divine provision, however, until the time of the Messiah, when God's original plan for Abraham, for his family and their "inheritance," would be fulfilled. Paul thus tells a layered narrative: Moses is vital and important, but not the final word, and the Torah was never intended as that final word. This was not a smooth progression, but nor was it simply a disaster, a bit of bad "religion" to be cleared out of the way to make room for the "revelation."

Romans 4 makes a similar but slightly different point. Like Galatians 3, Romans 4 picks up Genesis 15 in order to argue that now, in the Messiah, Israel's God has done what he always promised. He has created a family in which the nations would be included alongside Abraham's own physical offspring. But Paul has not forgotten the point which, as we already noted, might have been obvious to anyone reading Genesis 12 right after Genesis 1–11. The story of Abraham offers itself, in a canonical reading, as the "answer," the "solution," to the problem of Genesis 3–11. Many Jews in the Second-Temple period said something like this; it was not a new thing either when Paul said it or when a later Rabbi declared that God made Adam first, knowing that if he went wrong he could send Abraham to make it all better.

This relates to the larger biblical theme, which (granted) is not nearly so prominent in Second-Temple Jewish writings as it is in Paul: the idea of Israel as the "light to the nations." Isaiah 49, in which verse 6 is the explicit statement of that theme, is one of Paul's favourite chapters. But the idea is woven into the pattern of scripture at many points, not least in the Psalms: what Israel's God does for Israel is directly related to what, as creator, he will do in relation to the whole world. Sometimes what he will do for Israel is to condemn the wicked world. Sometimes he will bless the whole creation when the people of Israel worship him properly:

> May God be gracious to us and bless us
> and make his face to shine upon us,
> that your way may be known upon earth,
> your saving power among all nations. . . .
>
> Let the peoples praise you, O God;
> let all the peoples praise you.

> The earth has yielded its increase;
>> God, our God, has blessed us.
> May God continue to bless us;
>> let all the ends of the earth revere him.

(Psalm 67:1-2, 5-7)

There are literally dozens of other passages which either presuppose the same point (that what God does for Israel he does through Israel for the world, whether in judgment or in blessing) or make a similar one:

> God is king over the nations;
>> God sits on his holy throne.
> The princes of the peoples gather
>> as the people of the God of Abraham.
> For the shields of the earth belong to God;
>> he is highly exalted.

(Psalm 47:8-9)

And, in the passage from which Paul quotes, or to which he alludes, as often as he alludes to anything else:

> And now the Lord says, who formed me in the womb
> to be his servant,
>> to bring Jacob back to him, and that Israel might
>> be gathered to him,
>> for I am honored in the sight of the Lord, and
>> my god has become my strength—
> He says, "It is too light a thing that you should be my
> servant to raise up the tribes of Jacob
>> and to restore the survivors of Israel;
> I will give you as a light to the nations,
>> that my salvation may reach to the ends of the
>> earth."

(Isaiah 49:5-6)

As I said, it is quite true that one does not find these scriptural texts quoted very often in the regular literature of the
Second-Temple period. The idea that when God finally acts
to fulfil his promises to Israel then this, somehow, will take
account of the nations of the earth is, understandably perhaps,
cited more often in terms of a coming judgment on wicked
pagans than in terms of a coming blessing or ingathering.
But the texts are there, in Genesis, Deuteronomy, Isaiah, the
Psalms, and elsewhere; and Paul makes them central in his
evocation of the story which has led up to his gentile mission.
Once again, he is reading backwards: the texts already exist,
and he has known them and (in the case of the Psalms) prayed
them or sung them from his early youth. But something has
happened which has made him highlight this theme in a new
way. His explanation is obvious: it is the resurrection of the
crucified Messiah. If this is the eschatological moment for
which all Israel had been waiting (though without ever imagining that it would look like that!), then this must be the moment
for the pagans to be brought in at last; for the princes of the
people to be gathered into the people of the God of Abraham.
"Rejoice, you nations, with his people"; Romans 15:10, as we
saw earlier, quotes from another favourite passage, Deuteronomy 32 (in this case v. 43), as part of Paul's summary of the
theological exposition of his greatest letter.

The argument of Romans itself, seen as a whole, explains
how this works. (For this, one needs to adopt a reading strategy in which one sees the whole thing as a single unit, with
the parts meaning what they mean in relation to that whole.
Often exegesis is done differently, as though the parts had an
independent life, only tangentially related to their neighbour-
ing elements. This does not produce insight.) The argument
of Romans 5–8, highly complex though it is, arguably pivots
around the dense central passage of Romans 5:12-21, in which
Paul lines up Adam and the Messiah: the Messiah and his
obedience have accomplished, at last, not only the rescue of

"Adam" from sin, but also the reinstallation of humanity into its proper, divinely appointed, rule over creation:

> If, by the trespass of the one, death reigned through that one, how much more will those who receive the abundance of grace, and of the gift of covenant membership, of being "in the right," reign in life through the one man Jesus the Messiah.

(Romans 5:17)

Paul combines in this passage talk of the specific "sins" of Adam and his family with talk of Sin as a power, exercising its dominion through death. And the powers are defeated through the obedience of the Messiah.

Part of the point of Romans 5, however, is that it is both a summary of where the argument has got to by that point and a compressed advance statement of where it is going to as a result. From this mountain peak one can look back to chapters 1–4 and on to chapters 5–8, though of course, like Moses on Mount Pisgah, we can only glance in the present book at this view, not walk through the land for ourselves. The only point I want to make here, though it is a vital one, is that Paul has set out the Adam-Abraham link in the very structure of Romans. In Romans 4 he makes explicit the point which had been implicit ever since the announcement that in the gospel God's covenant faithfulness was revealed: God has done, in Jesus the Messiah, what he had always promised Abraham he would do. He has provided him with a worldwide family whose sole defining characteristic would be *pistis*, "faith" or "faithfulness." That is why, in chapter 5, Paul can declare that in the Messiah God has solved the Adam-problem. That is what the covenant with Abraham was there for in the first place. And this looks on to Romans 8, in which the "inheritance," which in Romans 4:13 is said to be "the world," is promised in more detail to the Messiah's people. The link here seems to be the messianic Psalm 2, where the promises to the Messiah are a worldwide extension of the promises to Abraham. God promised Abraham the land of Canaan, but to the Messiah he says,

> You are my son; today I have begotten you.
> Ask of me, and I will make the nations your heritage,
> and the ends of the earth your possession.

> (Psalm 2:7-8)

All the signs are that Paul had in his mind, as a result of what he believed about Jesus' resurrection, a fresh way of telling the familiar story: Adam, Abraham, Moses, Messiah. Moses could not be the means by which the ultimate Abraham-family would be created, or would inherit the larger possession. The Messiah has accomplished both.

All this sets up a context within which we can perhaps understand the more specific "doctrine of justification," which has loomed so large in so many debates in earlier centuries and again in our own day. The question I posed at the start of this chapter comes back to haunt us: when Paul speaks of "justification," does he refer to the "imputation" of the "righteousness of Christ" to the believer, or does he refer to the ingathering of the gentiles into the people of God?

It would be easy to answer, "Both": to line up various passages in which both seem to be said together (Romans 3 and 4, Galatians 2 and 3, Ephesians 2) and leave it at that. But this would be misleading. Both halves of the antithesis are in need of modification. I cannot repeat the detailed argument I have made elsewhere. I simply want to indicate how I think the land lies.

First, in the key passages the word "righteousness" is not used by Paul to mean a store of moral quality or virtue which the Messiah has as it were accumulated for himself and which can be accredited to the believer's account. This way of thinking of "justification" depends for its force on what has been

called a "covenant of works": God sets humans a moral challenge which they fail, incurring wrath, but Jesus succeeds in
their place and thus acquires on their behalf the moral bank
balance they lack. This theory, popular though it has been in
many quarters, is lacking both in semantic and exegetical pre-
cision and in theological coherence.

Second, when Paul speaks of the inclusion of gentiles in
the people of God, as part of what he means by "justification,"
this is much more than simply a matter of "table manners" in
which believing Jews are instructed to be courteous and wel-
coming to their believing gentile neighbours. Just as in more
traditional formulations, so here, what matters is the forgiveness of sins. The cross of the Messiah lies behind all Pauline
accounts of justification, and the particular point here is that
the gentiles are "sinners," as it were by definition, since they
are outside the Law. However, through the Messiah's cross,
believing gentiles are no longer "sinners." They have been forgiven. They can therefore be welcomed into the family. There
is no longer any bar on their membership.

That is what is going on in the complex argument of Galatians 2:15-21. Paul's riposte to Cephas at Antioch admitted
that the gentiles were "sinners" (2:15). But he went on to declare
that they had been welcomed in to God's people through the
faithfulness of the Messiah, who "loved me and gave himself
for me" (2:20), in other words, "who gave himself *for our sins*"
(1:4). The term Paul uses in 2:16 to denote that forgiving
welcome is "justification." Justification, for Paul, is "judicial"
or "forensic" in the sense that it is the *divine declaration* that
someone is "in the right"—and, since Paul's word *dikaiosynē*
carries more overtones than any word of ours can do, that such
a person is also "within the covenant." (Paul's notion that the
believer is also transformed by the work of the Spirit is a vital
ingredient within his larger picture, but, despite urging from
some quarters, I do not think it is part of the content of what
he means by "justification.") This justification takes place "in

the Messiah," as he says in 2:17, and also in Romans 3:24 and
Philippians 3:9. Schweitzer was correct (and so were those
Reformers, including John Calvin, who made the same point):
in Paul's own exposition, *"being in the Messiah" is the larger
idea, and "justification" is found within it.*

The idea of such a declaration, including particularly the
announcement that "gentile sinners" are able to be drawn in to
the family, is found also in Romans 4:1-8. The whole chapter
is about the fact that, in fulfilment of Genesis 15, Abraham's
family consists of "many nations," who are characterised by the
pistis which matches Abraham's own. Abraham is the father,
not of Jews only, but of the much larger family which God had
promised him—the promise which Abraham believed, on
the basis of which God established the covenant. The initial
promise concerned Abraham's enormous family; the covenant
promised them the land, and Paul, in line with the messianic
extension in Psalm 2, sees this as including the whole world
(4:13). How will this inclusion of gentile sinners come about?
Why, through the forgiveness of sins, of course: when God
promised Abraham that he would have a family like this, it
meant that God was promising to declare the "ungodly" gentiles to be "in the right," in the covenant, no longer "sinners"
because their sins had been forgiven.

Paul has already explained in Romans 3:24-26 how sins
are forgiven through the Messiah's faithful death. He has
already explained in 3:27-30 that, on this basis, believing Jews
and believing gentiles are declared to be members of God's single family, with their defining mark being the *pistis*, "faith" or
"faithfulness," which reflects the *pistis* of the Messiah himself
(3:22), "in whom" they are then justified (3:24). Now, in chapter 4, he explains that this is in direct fulfilment of the divine
promises to Abraham, so that in chapter 5 he can declare
that through the Messiah God has at last provided the solution to the problem of Adam. This then forms the platform
for the exposition of the full restoration of humanity in the

resurrection within the restored creation, the ultimate Abrahamic "inheritance," in chapter 8. And this then, in ways too complex to consider here, necessarily points on to the agonised though finally celebratory wrestlings of chapters 9–11 and the bracing instructions, not least the instructions for Jewish Christians and gentile Christians to worship together, in chapters 12–16.

Though this discussion has been necessarily brief, I hope it will serve to indicate the lay of the land. Paul's vision of the people of God cannot be reduced to terms either of "a company of saved sinners" or "the replacement for Israel." We must see it, instead, in terms of *the Messiah himself*, the one who, being raised from the dead, embodies in himself the destiny and vocation of Israel, to be the light of the nations. This is neither an un-Jewish nor an anti-Jewish vision. It is a classically first-century Jewish vision of Israel, focused on its anointed king. What nobody in that world had imagined before, but what could only be imagined from within that world, on the basis of the shocking new revelation of the resurrection of the crucified Messiah, was that through those events the people of God would be radically redefined as those who died to their former identities and rose again into the new messianic life. "In the Messiah," then, they became a single family, whose one and only badge of membership was *pistis*, their faithful allegiance to the one God of Israel who had revealed himself as the God who raised Jesus from the dead and appointed him as Lord of the whole world. It was scandalous then. For some, it is scandalous still.

The Lordship of Jesus over the whole world forms the foundation of Paul's missionary theology, and therefore also—since he saw that mission as part of his own vocational self-understanding—of his theological method. It is to these topics that we turn in our final chapter.

5

THEOLOGY, MISSION, AND METHOD

Paul's and Ours

Everybody knows that Paul was a missionary. But what was the dynamic of this mission? Since the word "mission" has currency in today's world, people easily assimilate what he says and does into one or other of the two main models. They can be characterised like this:

> **a. Was Paul's "mission" a matter of saving as many "souls" as he could from the wreck of the world and the wrath of God?**

It is probably true that many of the "missions" launched from the western churches in the last three hundred years had something like this as their aim. But that is not the only possible meaning:

> **b. Was Paul's "mission" a matter, rather, of infiltrating the culture of his day, transforming it steadily from within?**

It has often been assumed, I think, that Paul's "mission" was of the first rather than the second type. And there are several signs that something like this was the case. Paul refers to those who will, and those who will not, "inherit God's kingdom." He distinguishes between "those who are perishing" and "those who are saved." He warns Christian spouses not to be too quick to write off an unbelieving spouse; perhaps they may after all be saved. There is much more like this. He instructs the Corinthians to eject from the assembly the man who has committed incest, so that, while the satan can have his body his spirit may be saved at the day of the Lord Jesus. Workers who have produced shoddy work will find that work burnt up on "the Day," while they themselves will be saved, but only as through a fire. And so on. It is easy to conclude from all this that Paul fits the very model of a modern-style evangelist, urging people to believe and so to be saved, warning Christians that they must continue to live "in the Messiah" since other roads lead to death. He even says of himself that he has to keep his body firmly in place lest, after preaching to others, he himself might be cast away.

One particular, but unsettling, example of this is the famous phrase, which we approached from another angle in the previous chapter: "All Israel shall be saved" (Romans 11:26). This is not the moment for a full-dress exposition of that phrase, the climax of the long and difficult argument that began in chapter 9. But that is part of the point. The reason the argument is long and difficult is that Paul cannot say, at the start of chapter 9, that one need not worry about presently unbelieving Jews since he knows they will all be saved in the end. All the signs are that in Romans 9–11 Paul is not "thinking on his feet," musing his way through a dark subject, trying this line and that until finally discovering a happy ending. The section is extremely carefully structured and balanced. Paul knows the end from the beginning. *And the beginning is agonising.* He has "great sorrow and endless pain" in his heart. He prays fervently to God about his fellow Jews, "for their salvation" (10:1). And in 10:9 he explains what the answer is, an answer rooted in his exposition of Deuteronomy 30: "if you profess with your mouth that Jesus is Lord, and believe in your heart that God raised him from the dead, you will be saved." It could hardly be clearer.

Either, then, Paul has simply changed his mind about salvation by the end of chapter 11, or he should, after writing 11:26, have told Tertius to strike out the previous two chapters. No need for anguish or intercession; they will all be saved anyway. But actually chapter 11 is also clear, looking back to chapter 10: "if they do not remain in unbelief," the presently unbelieving Jews will be grafted back in (11:23).

But we must notice what Paul does not say in chapter 11. He does not say that he is coming to Rome to engage in evangelism among his Jewish kinsfolk. Nor does he suggest that the Roman Christians should try their hand at such a mission. Rather, on the basis of Deuteronomy 32, he says that God will make unbelieving Israel "jealous": jealous "with a non-nation." His gentile apostolate itself has this as one of its prime, though oblique, objects: "to make 'my flesh' jealous, and save some of them" (Romans 11:14). The "some" here reminds us, inevitably, of 1 Corinthians 9:22: Paul has become "all things to all people, so that in all ways I might save some." Paul, a master of the rhetorically well-turned phrase, either went to sleep on the job, meaning to write "all" but for some reason missing the chance, or he was being realistic about what can and cannot, what will and will not, be done. But when it comes to his fellow Jews, not least in Rome, Paul seems to be forswearing any direct method. He is praying to God for his kinsfolk. "God is able to graft them back in" (Romans 11:23), but Paul has no immediate plans to be the instrument of that divine action. His word to the Roman Christians is not that they should do so, either; only that they should be prepared for it to happen, and not engage in what we now know to be a proto-Marcionite anti-Jewish rejection, as though the Jesus-movement, having begun with Jews, is now only for gentiles. For Paul, that would be the ultimate anti-Judaism: not the hope for them to recognise Jesus as their Messiah, but the determination that they should not. There are many things here to unsettle and destabilise modern notions of mission.

This points to a larger world of Pauline "mission" which forms the hinterland of Paul's gentile apostolate. This has some analogies with the second possibility highlighted at the start of this chapter, but it is interestingly different. Here what matters is Paul's doctrine of *creation and new creation*. His work, founding communities loyal to Jesus and learning to think messianically, was designed to produce signs of new creation in the middle of the old world—the old world which was, though old and decaying, still the good creation of the good creator. It can therefore be argued that, as he says in 2 Corinthians 10, his mission envisages both confrontation and cooptation:

> We tear down clever arguments and every proud notion that sets itself up against the knowledge of God. We take every thought prisoner and make it obey the Messiah.
>
> (2 Corinthians 10:4-5)

The world is full of folly but also of good and useful things— good and useful, that is, if they can be liberated from the enslaving thought-forms and life-ways of the pagan world and brought into the new-creation world of the gospel.

We can see Paul working this out in all the major spheres of life. His communities are to be united and loyal to Jesus in a world where Caesar would love to have brought such multicoloured groups into a single loyalty to himself. His financial arrangements in the churches, especially his concern for the poor, and his "collection" from the gentile churches to support the Jewish church in Jerusalem, were a sign of a different pattern of social and economic life, designed not as a private club but as a new way of living. His articulation of the new creation, and the new ethics and epistemology that went with it, formed a rich mixture of challenge and cooptation, much like his reported speech on the Areopagus in Acts 17. Paul's churches, small and embattled as they often were, must often have felt as though they were a tiny protest movement, living out a strange, difficult and radically different life with the rest of the world taking no notice except for the occasional persecution. But that was not Paul's idea. For Paul, these communities were embodying *a new way of being human*, the new-creation way in which everything good in the old creation would be enhanced and everything corrupt and wicked in the old creation would be left behind.

We see the balance in a delightful verse in Philippians, one of the most obvious letters for this confrontation-and-cooptation position:

> For the rest, my dear family, these are the things you should think through: whatever is true, whatever is holy, whatever is upright, whatever is pure, whatever is attractive, whatever has a good reputation; anything virtuous, anything praiseworthy. And these are the things you should do: what you learned, received, heard, and saw in and through me. And the God of peace will be with you.

> (Philippians 4:8-9)

There are many things in the world of creation that can be celebrated; the Philippian church should not hide away from the world and pretend that they and they alone have the monopoly on wisdom or virtue. But there is a single, narrow, clearly defined way to behave: Paul has modeled it, they have observed it, God will be with them if they follow it. Here is the balance. The new creation bursts in upon the old, but when it sees the old, and when the old sees it, there should be a recognition:

the one is not the abolition, but the renewal, of the other. Of course, the renewal takes place, like all renewals in the gospel, through death and resurrection. Hence the persecution, hence too the moral struggle and challenge. But Paul does not retreat. The new creation is the reality which has already come to birth in the resurrection of Jesus, and which forms the model for, and the means toward, the ultimate goal.

These brief reflections about Paul's mission raise a very different sort of question which needs to be addressed, a question of method, both Paul's and ours. It is vital to distinguish six things which are not always, or indeed often, distinguished.

1. First, how did Paul himself arrive at his beliefs and ideas? This subdivides further: what was the initial impulse, and what were the further impulses that shaped the ideas as they formed?

2. Second, how did Paul, left to himself, line up the beliefs to which he came? Did he do that at all, or were his thoughts simply a rich and muddled mixture of scripture and spirituality, of prejudice and philosophy, jostling around and ready to spill out into another lecture, another sermon, another letter?

3. Third, what train of thought does Paul use in explaining or teaching those ideas to his hearers? Here again we might want to distinguish at least two things. Letters and seminars are not the same thing. Paul may well have used quite different methods in arguing things out in person to those he used when composing a sustained piece of writing designed to be read straight through.

Already we must note the radical difference between (1) and (3). People sometimes used to suggest that Paul was inconsistent since the arguments he was using do not express the ways in which he himself had arrived at his views. This is naive. There are many ways you can arrive at a belief, and these may or may not be the same route by which one makes a convincing argument. I may know, for a thousand reasons, that my granddaughter was born in 2005, but if I turn up at the airport check-in desk without her passport the clerk will pay no attention to these reasons, and continue to demand documentation. The evidence which, for one person, merely confirms something that is known in much deeper ways may be the one solid thing another person can hang on to. And, in between (1) and (3), the evidence does actually suggest that for Paul (2) was important as well. There are many times when he says something in one letter, clipped and bare almost to the point of incomprehensibility, which he explains much more fully in another letter.

This suggests strongly that when he wrote, though he may well have had new thoughts as he did so (that happens, as writers know, no matter how well you know your subject or plan in advance), the basic outline of his beliefs about God, God's people, and God's future was firmly in place, and that he could draw on these large topics, and those that nested within them, in different ways for different rhetorical purposes. Thus, just as Paul is not "inconsistent" if we catch him out mounting an argument which, from all the evidence available, does not seem to be the way by which he himself reached that position, so he is not "inconsistent" if the rhetorical needs of the Corinthian situation lead him to draw upon his larger stock of thought-through ideas and present certain elements in one way while the rhetorical needs of the Thessalonian church lead him to draw upon that same larger stock and present it in a different way. The eschatological vision of 1 Thessalonians 4:15-18 is actually referring to the same moment as 1 Corinthians 15:51-54, but it comes out quite differently. This is not a sign that Paul has changed his mind. In fact, it is clear that he has not. Nor do these passages give us access to "how Paul arrived

at this in the first place." That is not the point. His theological pilgrimage, we know, came about because of the explosive
effect of meeting the crucified and risen Jesus on the heart,
mind, and life of someone believing the sort of things he had
believed before and living in the way he had lived before. The
radical, "apocalyptic" transformation was a transformation of
those beliefs and *that* life, not some other.

When, therefore, we study Paul, it is not only appropriate but actually necessary to keep these levels in mind all the
time, and to be prepared constantly to distinguish them. This
applies particularly, as so much does, to the study of Romans
and its relationship to the larger world of Paul's thought. It so
happens that the rhetorical needs of the Roman situation, as
Paul saw it, called forth one particular presentation. And it
so happens that this particular presentation has resonated so
strongly with some movements in Christian history that it has
been easy to make the mistake of thinking that Romans is a
"straightforward" presentation of "Paul's gospel." It has also
been easy to react against this and to declare that only part
of Romans really represents "what Paul really thought." The
distinction I have been making ought to help us refrain from
either sort of hasty judgment.

This brings us, however, to the same set of questions as
applied to ourselves, only this time, since our subject matter
has been Paul's thinking, these three questions must be
related, in so far as we can do so, to each question we have
asked of Paul.

4. Fourth, then, how did we ourselves come to read
    Paul in the way that we now do? How did we
    arrive at a conclusion about his starting point, his
    overall and settled theology, and his situationally
    distinct rhetorical strategies?
5. What kind of settled picture have we now formed
    of Paul as a whole, to the three Pauline questions

above? How does this picture relate to the process investigated under (4)? How does this settled picture (always, to be sure, like any scientific
construct, under constant revision) emerge in
our reading of particular letters, and enable us to
address particular issues?

6. How do we choose a rhetorical strategy by which
to persuade others that our view of Paul, his starting point, his settled theology, and his particular
rhetorical aims in particular letters, are to be
preferred as historically sound and theologically
coherent arguments? How are we best to present
our findings?

We note, as with the similar questions about Paul, that
these three steps are very different. I may have been taught a
particular view of Paul by a favourite teacher, but if I want to
argue for that view to someone else, it will not help to say, "I
really liked the teacher who showed me this." The way I came
to an initial view of Paul may be very different to the way I
then developed a larger picture of his world and his thought.
Neither way will necessarily be anything like the way in which
I might need to present an argument for a particular interpretation either of his starting point, or of his "big picture," or of
his argument in one particular letter. Indeed, there will always
be a danger of confusion between the attempt to track Paul's
own thought and the attempt to follow through my own interpretation of him. The process of enquiry will need to go back
and forwards between all these levels, all the time.

Here we face a difficulty. The supposed "scientific" dom-
inance of the western academy has, over the last many years,
tended to privilege the method known as "induction." Here
is a text: what can we learn from it? What can we infer from
it? This is a ground-up method: we start with the fragments
and we clean them up, hoping perhaps that some of them will

fit together but not worrying too much if they don't, or not yet. Some scholarly personalities are strongly attracted to this kind of approach, and get very twitchy about anyone imposing other ideas as it were from above. A famous recent book (Iain McGilchrist, *The Master and His Emissary* [New Haven, Conn.: Yale University Press, 2009]) has argued that the western world in general has become more and more inclined to discount "right-brain" thinking (imagination, "big picture" thinking, strategy) and to privilege "left-brain" thought instead (studying details, sorting out small bits of the puzzle). That broad-brush summary does not do justice to the detail either of the book or of the brain science which stands behind it, but the picture is all too familiar. However, whatever "big picture" one may propose, using the "master" right hemisphere of the brain, it is vital that the details are scrutinised rigorously with the left hemisphere. It is the awkward details, the ones which don't quite fit the big picture, that are the likely points of growth, of modifying hypotheses or perhaps abandoning them and getting better ones instead.

In particular, those who read texts and use "induction" to do so are likely to get worried, with good reason, at any suggestion of a grand scheme, whether theological, sociological, or whatever, which tries to tell them what "must have" been the case, what something "must have" meant. This is "deduction." One meets it, for instance, when a recent theologian says that Romans 3:24-26 "must be" eucharistic, or an anthropologist says that because most people in the ancient Mediterranean world were functionally illiterate, Jesus "could not" have read the scriptures in the synagogue in Nazareth, or a devout Roman Catholic theologian tells me that when Jesus was raised from the dead, he "must have" gone first to see his mother, even though no texts record this supposed fact.

The problem is, of course, that "induction," taken strictly, only gets you so far. Every play we watch, every novel we read, invites us, nudges us, hints at us that there is a larger framework, a bigger meaning, than the scatter of apparently unrelated details would "prove" of themselves. We are trying to work out "what is going on." We make guesses; perhaps he really had known her many years before, perhaps her mother really had seen him in church that day, perhaps there was a dark family secret that explains the odd behaviour that night after the party. And so on. As we move on, hypotheses get tested against more evidence. It is a constant to-and-fro. And, in the classic Sherlock Holmes model, we have "abduction," the "inference to the best explanation." Philosophers have refined these, but the overall task is clear. You start with a rigorous study of the basic material. You form a hypothesis about how it all fits. You bring that back to the data. It doesn't quite fit. You try it again, perhaps in consultation with colleagues. You discover data in another adjacent field which seems to be relevant, and try out various hypotheses to include that as well in a new picture, always coming back to the primary data under consideration. And so on. In that sequence, it is again and again and the bits of evidence that don't quite fit that nudge you once more into a further refined hypothesis. This is how reading works. It is how history works. It is how exegesis works.

The problem is that those who know the importance of induction as the safeguard against fantasy—those, in other words, who insist on sticking to the letter of the text and seldom moving far from it—always tend to see "abduction" coming down the road and suppose that it is "deduction" in sheep's clothing. They hear a hypothesis that has in fact been through the mill of many years' testing against the detailed evidence, that has been modified or clarified in the process (pretty much, in fact, what the physicist or the astronomer would do), and they assume that this is a heavy-handed "deduction" from an a priori scheme. It thus becomes very difficult to persuade others that the new hypothesis has been arrived at by the combination of induction (ruthless attention to the details of the text), inference to the best explanation (finding a model which explains why the writer would have wanted to say just this, in this way, at this point), and the checking and refining which has gone on because the first version of the hypothesis still left some data out of consideration, still did not quite fit all the quirky bits of the text.

The guild of New Testament scholars has developed, over the years, a fairly standard way of presenting arguments. This applies not only to the writing of dissertations, but to monographs and similar projects. First you state the problem in your chosen early Christian text, mapping out the current scholarship as best you can. Then you investigate the larger framework, particularly the Greco-Roman and Jewish worlds, which might help in the understanding of this text. Then you return to your text, and your question, to see what new light may have been shed. This is a tried and tested method. The alternative—and one shudders to think of it—is that every time you hit a question, in Romans or John or Revelation or wherever, you should break off from discussing the text itself and insert a fifty-page excursus about the wider context. That would be like attending a dinner party at which, every time a guest asked a question, the host made a half-hour phone call to a friend to check on the correct answer. For the same reason, biblical commentators regularly insert an excursus on a key topic at an early point in the work, to save having to say everything all over again the next time the same topic comes up. In the nature of the case, an early excursus on (say) the identity of the "teachers" in Galatia will draw on material from later on in the book, even though the later passage has not yet been discussed in the commentary proper. Alternatively, someone writing a book on a major theme in Paul, or John, or Matthew, or whoever is very likely to expound the theme itself as the main road through the project, with excursuses in which the key texts can be dealt with once, thoroughly, rather than over and over again.

Most people who read scholarly monographs take all this for granted. They know that the best way to present the evidence is to gather up into a coherent account of the wider context all the material that may then be relevant later on, that will assist in forming the "best explanation" for the text. The fact that it is presented first within the rhetorical shape of the monograph does not mean that it was all decided up front, before the text was even considered. Nor does such a preliminary scene-setting exercise pretend to be anything other than what it is, a study of material which, from careful study of the basic text, has a good prima facie claim to be considered relevant. Of course, it is always possible that such a treatment will turn into a major "deductive" scheme. That has happened. Here is a hypothetical first-century Gnostic redeemer myth; let us suppose that it explains the rise of early Christian thought. Here is an anthropological analysis of "the Mediterranean world"; let us apply it to the New Testament and see what was "really" going on. And so on. But the answer to this is not, Let us have no large hypotheses, but, Let us relentlessly and ruthlessly check every hypothesis back against the raw data of the text.

Of course, no interpreter ever comes to the text with a tabula rasa. Until quite recently, the great majority of readers of Paul, and particularly Romans, assumed without question that he was addressing the questions which the western church was addressing when it discussed "justification." He was (it was assumed) discussing "how to get saved": is it "by works" or "by faith," and, if the latter, what shall I do next, now that I have believed? That larger narrative loomed so massively over discussions that people were able to assume it wasn't even there, that they were just "reading the text." It was, of course, always vulnerable to the charge that there were bits of Paul, and again particularly of Romans, which didn't fit. Romans 9–11, notoriously, had to be left out, and various ingenious strategies were developed to that end. This is not the place to discuss that question itself. I only mention it to show that all those who read Paul are in fact making "inferences to (what they hope is) the best explanation," all the time. The way to guard against "deduction," and the false schemes it produces, is not to abandon "abduction," but to be aware of how it works.

The result of all this is that writers and readers alike must carefully distinguish between abduction and deduction. It will not do, when faced with an abductive hypothesis which itself grew out of inductive study of relevant material, to assume that it is in fact a deduction and to suggest that the writer is bringing to the text an alien or home-made interpretative grid which then forces the text to stand on its hind legs and dance a jig. Faced with that kind of charge, one possible response would be to point out that this is in fact what has happened all along as the interpretative grids of various western soteriologies have been imposed on Paul, screening out some integral parts of his thought and over-emphasising others. It will not do, at that point, to object that the western readings have just been reading the text without any controlling presuppositions. The days of such naivety are past. The answer to any new proposal for an "inference to the best explanation," whether it be an anthropological theory, a theological insight, a fresh reading of Paul's Roman culture or his Jewish context, or anything else, is not to wave it away because it upsets the way one has always read the text. The answer, as with the Jews in Beroea in Acts 17, is to search the evidence carefully to see whether these things might be so. And, in particular, to look back at the original text to see if the fresh interpretation clarifies things that before were unclear, and to apply all the usual tests of a hypothesis: to get in the data, to do so with appropriate simplicity, and to shed light if possible on other cognate areas of research.

One of the key parts of the formation of hypotheses, equally true for physics or geology as well as for literature or the history of art, is the *imagination*. Back to the right brain once more. Hypotheses designed to explain the data are not usually themselves arrived at by pure, plodding induction. They require an imaginative leap—which then immediately requires more detailed study of the evidence, "to see whether these things are so." In this whole process, therefore, history in general and exegesis as a specific branch of history ought to welcome insights from the arts, and perhaps even the use of art as a framing device. It is, again, characteristic of the modern western period that art has been regarded as "the pretty bit around the border" which can then be dispensed with when the real work begins. That is a dangerous truncation of the process. It is not a guarantee that one will avoid airy, fluffy hypotheses; it merely increases the probability that one's hypotheses will be more like a brutalist block of flats in a Soviet-era city than a well-designed, elegant street of houses. Elegance is seen as a virtue in physics; why not in exegesis as well?

Review Citations

Barclay, J. M. G. *Scottish Journal of Theology* 68, no. 2 (May 2015): 235–43.

Bockmuehl, Markus. *Journal for the Study of Paul and His Letters* 4, no. 1 (Spring 2014): 59–70.

de Boer, Martinus. *Journal for the Study of Paul and His Letters* 4, no. 1 (Spring 2014): 49–58.

Brown, Alexandra. *The Christian Century* 131, no. 22 (October 29, 2014): 37–39.

Campbell, Douglas A. *Marginalia* (January 6, 2015). http://marginalia.lareviewofbooks.org/douglas-campbell/, accessed April 21, 2015.

Dunn, James D. G. *Journal of Theological Studies* 66, no. 1 (April 2015): 408–14.

Fredriksen, Paula. *Catholic Biblical Quarterly* 77, no. 2 (April 2015): 387–91.

Gathercole, Simon. *Reformation 21* (July 2014). http://www.reformation21.org/articles/paul-and-the-faithfulness-of-god-a-review.php, accessed April 21, 2015.

Gaventa, Beverly R. *Journal for the Study of Paul and His Letters* 4, no. 1 (Spring 2014): 71–80.

Gorman, Michael. *Journal for the Study of Paul and His Letters* 4, no. 1 (Spring 2014): 27–36.

Hailes, Sam. *Christian Today* (January 24, 2014). http://www.christiantoday.com/article/new.testament.scholar.nt.wright.on.paul.and.the.faithfulness.of.god/35533.htm, accessed April 21, 2015.

Hurtado, Larry. *Theology* 117, no. 5 (September/October 2014): 361–65.

Moo, Douglas. *The Gospel Coalition* (November 6, 2013). http://www.thegospelcoalition.org/article/paul_and_the_faithfulness_of_god, accessed April 21, 2015.

Schreiner, Thomas. *Journal for the Study of Paul and His Letters* 4, no. 1 (Spring 2014): 1–26.

Starling, David. *Journal for the Study of Paul and His Letters* 4, no. 1 (Spring 2014): 37–48.

Tilling, Chris. *ANVIL: Anglican Evangelical Journal for Theology and Mission* 31, no. 1 (March 2015): 45–69.